TRANSFORMING
FAITH
to Shape the World Around Us

D1407913

REGINALD F. DAVIS

© 2019

Published in the United States by Nurturing Faith Inc., Macon GA,

www.nurturingfaith.net.

Library of Congress Cataloging-in-Publication Data is available.

ISBN:978-1-63528-072-2

Cover photo by BlackJack3D.

DEDICATION

I would like to acknowledge the support and prayers of the
Davis family while writing this book. I want to thank my
brother James Davis, Jr. for proof reading the text. Also, I want
to thank my wife Myrlene Davis and our three children for their
prayers and support. Special thanks to the Lord for giving me the
mind and the opportunity to encourage and enlighten the Body
of Christ concerning faith. Also, special thanks to the Nurturing
Faith team for accepting this work for publication. Their support
and suggestions have been invaluable.

CONTENTS

INTRODUCTION

With God, you are stronger than your struggles and
more fierce than your fears.

—Germany Kent

We possess tremendous power as children of God. God knew we would need power to have dominion over his creation. God placed us in a position of power to govern the earth as heaven is governed. We are the reflection of God on earth—the eyes, feet, tongue, arms, and legs of God. God put within us the power to manage his creation and gave us the authority to govern earth with his backing. We were put in the position of stewardship, not ownership, in a covenant relationship with the God. This exalted position was given to us only as trustees because "the earth is the LORD's and the fullness thereof, the world and those who dwell therein" (Ps 24:1).

Our stewardship comes with responsibility. Whatever goes on in the earth realm, it is our responsibility to allow it or reject it. We have the authority to say yes or no. The ontological question is "What happened in reality that caused chaos to threaten our highest good?" Traditional theology says we willfully allowed sin (the opposite of our highest good) to enter into the equation between God and humanity, which had ethical and ontological consequences. We lost our power and authority and became servants of sin: "Man's sin destroyed the creation covenant and fractured his relationship with the Creator. Because God loved man, however, He provided a means by which man could be restored to a right relationship: the covenant of redemption."[1] For hundreds of centuries, Satan and the demons—the promoters of sin—reigned over humanity with a maniacal hatred until the Son of God, Jesus Christ, came along and defeated him on the cross: "Having disarmed the powers and authorities, he made a public spectacle of them, triumphing over them by the cross" (Col 2:15). As a result Christ returned to us the stewardship and relationship we lost by sin. We once again have been empowered and given authority by faith to do God's will on earth.

Therefore, since Christ publicly defeated sin, death, and the grave, our faith can no longer be a private matter. We must engage society for its transformation. Christ's ministry was public. The power Jesus demonstrated to heal the sick, raise the dead, feed the hungry, open up blinded eyes, cut loose stammering tongues, and perform all kinds of miracles was public, and we must share our faith as Jesus did. Jesus said, "Behold, I have given you the authority to trample on snakes and scorpions, and to overcome all the power of the enemy; nothing will harm you" (Luke 10:19). Because of what Christ did on Calvary, we have what it takes to redeem the evil times in which we live. "The Spirit who gave Daniel his wisdom, and Isaiah his eloquence, and Jeremiah his tenacity, and Amos his holy indignation, can equip us with power, even you and me, for there is no exception."[2]

Shame on us if we don't use the power and authority God has given us through Jesus. We are a paragon of possibilities through Christ. God takes our moral failures and mistakes and turns them into miracle-working power to transform the world. So if you have messed up in life and think your life is over, you are more in line with biblical characters than you think. The scriptures are replete with people who messed up, screwed up, were twisted up, tied up, and tangled up. But through the creative redemptive power and grace of God, these same people obtained supernatural results because they put faith in the one greater than themselves. The power they allowed to operate in and through them by faith is available to us today. So don't think biblical characters were endowed with special characteristics that we don't have. Since faith is a gift of God (Eph 2:8–9), biblical characters have no advantage over us in receiving this faith imputed to us through grace. "If we exercise our faith as they did we will also experience similar triumphs as they enjoyed, for it is God's desire that we do so, which is why He graced us with this precious gift."[3] We all have the same endowment; we are human just as Jesus Christ was human.

What made Jesus such a great and powerful personality was "God was in Christ reconciling the world to Himself, not counting their trespasses against them, and He has committed to us the word of reconciliation" (2 Cor 5:19). What God accomplished through Christ can be done through us if we allow God to live in us by faith. It is not enough to believe in God. We must act on our belief by faith to transform the world. The world doesn't measure our belief; the world measures the actions we take and the results we get based upon our faith. Moses may not be well known for the rod in his hand, but he is known for splitting the Red Sea. We may not know the wife of Joshua, but we do know that through faith, Joshua caused the sun to stand still. It may not matter to us that David was the last child of Jesse, but it does matter that by faith he stood up to an intimidating giant called Goliath and destroyed him. Albert Einstein may not be known for being a violin player, but he is known for developing the theory of relativity. The world looks at results, not creeds, but deeds that produce results.

The same faith that Moses, Joshua, David, Jesus, Einstein, and others throughout human history demonstrated to show the power of God to transform the world is the same enormous power scientists call the "big bang." Think about the billions of galaxies that were formed from this enormous power; think about the planets that were formed as a result of this enormous power. Once we look in space and see the stars, the moon, and the planets that orbit around the sun held together by an unseen energy called gravity, we have to conclude that enormous power brought all of this together in one amazing order. God is this power, and we have this enormous creative power available to us, which can only be activated by faith: "By faith we understand that the worlds were framed by the word of God, so that the things which are seen were not made of things which are visible" (Heb 11:3). Just like the planets orbit around the sun for their power, when we orbit around the Son of God by faith, we have power to achieve amazing things. Since God has put mankind as manager over the work of His hand, anything that needs correcting is his responsibility. Martin Buber, the Jewish existentialist, stated, "Man can choose God and he can reject God.... That man has the power to lead the world to perdition implies that he has power to lead the world to redemption.... These two powers of man constitute the actual admission of man into mightiness.... The fact remains that the creation of this being, man, means that God has made room for a codetermine power, for a starting-point for events."[4]

This tremendous power within humanity must be accessed by faith in order to rise to our God-given potential and purpose. God and humans acting together can transform the world. To achieve this, there must be a covenant relationship between God and humans to help us not lead the world to perdition as Martin Buber indicated. God loves us so much that God *became* us. Harvey Cox stated,

> Yahweh was willing to stoop so low as to work in tandem with man, to work on a team, no matter how poorly the human partner was working out. It can certainly be said that in Jesus of Nazareth God did show that he was willing to take man's side of the unfilled covenant, to be the junior partner in the asymmetrical relationship. He who is '"high and lifted up"' suggests that...he is willing to put himself in the position of working within a group.... The idea of an I–You relationship between God and man is strongly hinted by the language of Galatians 4.... Man's relationship derives from the work they do together.[5]

Whatever is accomplished on earth through this partnership between God and humans means that humans must always be expected to do their part and follow God as recipients of the covenant of grace. Karl Barth said, "God is the giver and man the recipient. Man is an active, not an inactive recipient, yet even in his activity he is still a recipient. In the present context the decisive point is that God directs, demands, orders, and commands, while man can exercise his responsibility only by obeying God's command."[6]

Therefore, there is no excuse for humanity to allow the decimation of themselves and the planet when they possess so much power through Christ Jesus our Lord. Our failure to act to oppose wrong, evil, and injustice is the result of unfaithfulness. Obedience to God is always required to accomplish God's will on earth. Obedience is

> an action that characterizes the event of the Christian life. It controls it in all its dimensions. In it man as a Christian acquires his freedom, and in it consists the exercise of this freedom: his conversion and decision. It is the work of his faith and gratitude. His faithfulness is his persistence in the repetition of this action. It is the epitome and common denominator of all that the gracious God expects and wants of man and all that comes into question as man's obedience to the gracious God. God commands this action, and in performing it man does what is right and good before him.[7]

A. W. Tozer reminds us that "the Bible recognizes no faith that does not lead to obedience, nor does it recognize any obedience that does not spring from faith. The two are opposite sides of the same coin. Were we to split a coin edgewise we would destroy both sides and render the whole thing valueless. So faith and obedience are forever joined and each one is without value when separated from the other."[8]

Jesus Christ was in a persistent relationship with God: "He humbled himself by becoming obedient to death—even death on a cross" (Phil 2:8). We are expected by faith to do likewise if we desire to transform the world as Jesus did. The disciples were able to perform miracles because they were in relationship with Jesus Christ. God's tremendous power was released through them, causing an explosions of miracles to happen among them. We can do the same thing in our time. Scripture says that people laid the sick in the streets that "Peter's shadow might fall on some of them as he passed by...and all of them were healed" (Acts 5:15–16). People had faith in the shadow of Peter because they perceived that Peter and John had been with Jesus (Acts 4:13). It wasn't the shadow of Peter that healed the people, nor was it the hair on Samson's head that gave him supernatural strength. It was the power of God channeled through these human vessels by faith to achieve amazing results.

Power companies have power lines running to our homes and businesses; however, it is up to us to turn on the switch to access the power. It doesn't matter the size or the location of our homes and businesses; we have the same power running to them. So it is with faith. Faith is the switch that accesses this enormous power through us. It doesn't matter our race, creed, color, tongue, or nationality; the same faith is available to us all. When we flip the switch of faith in our individual and collective lives, power is released and amazing things take place. The ordinary becomes the extraordinary; the simple becomes the supernatural; the unknown becomes the well-known. God through Christ can use anybody regardless of their limitations to bring glory to his name. However, none of this is possible without putting faith in action.

When we act by faith, God releases his power of transformation to bring liberation, restoration, and reconciliation in a divided and torn situation. God is the power; we are the instruments through which this power is made manifest on earth. God uses our hands, feet, eyes, and tongue to accomplish his work on earth. We must never forget that we are the instruments and transmitters and God is the power. In any situation and circumstance, when we act on our faith in God, the dam of heaven is open and the power of God rushes down to aid us. "It is faith in [God] that we must rediscover. With this faith we can transform bleak and desolate valleys into sunlit paths of joy and bring new light into the dark caverns of pessimism."[9]

Just as God achieved amazing things through characters in the Bible, God can do the same through us. The characters in the Bible were flawed—suffering from defects, deficiencies, and disadvantages as we do—but God has proven he is still willing to achieve great things in and through us. All we have to do is open up ourselves to God by faith. When Jacob opened up himself by faith, he was transformed from Jacob to Israel. When Rahab opened up herself by faith, she moved from being a harlot to heroine. When Simon of sand opened up himself by faith, he became Peter the rock. When persecuting Saul opened himself up by faith, he became the apostle Paul.

There are many within the "hall of faith" who opened up themselves by faith to be used by the power of God. By faith God is calling us to do the possible; God will do the impossible. Therefore, there is no excuse for us allowing our society and nation to be in a perpetual state of nihilism when we have tremendous power at our disposal. Could it be that Jesus Christ may cast us in utter darkness for not using the talents given to us to bring transformation to our world? Our lack of faith in God and in our abilities to transform the world around us is robbing the kingdom of heaven of souls and God of his glory in the world.

God is not asking us to have everything figured out before we act by faith. We may never understand how God achieves great things. We may never comprehend the complexities of God's ways. But we must trust God in all things and have faith and put this faith in action. We are not expected to waste our time on earth trying to figure out an infinite God, for we are finite creatures. Isaiah reminds us, "God's thoughts are not our thoughts nor God's ways our ways. For as the heavens are higher than the earth, so are God's ways higher than our ways and thoughts than our thoughts" (Isa 55:8–9). Despite our limited understanding of an infinite God, acting on our faith in God can yield amazing results.

Too often we fail in achieving great things on earth because our faith in God is missing in action. We put faith in the government, in our economy, in institutions that often fail us. Using human strength and knowledge alone to get supernatural results is impossible. Remember, Samson, who disobeyed God and gave the secret of his strength to Delilah, did not know that the Lord had left him (Judg 16:20). When God left Samson, he no longer possessed supernatural strength to defeat his enemies. When we have God as our divine partner and this partnership is persistent, God gives us supernatural power to achieve things for his glory. Not only does God give us supernatural strength, but "God gives life to the dead and calls those things which do not exist as though they did" (Rom 4:17). Partnership with God makes all the difference in the world. Jesus said, "Without me you can do nothing" (John 15:5). Trying to impact and transform the world without the power of God is futile. It is like trying to blow down an oak tree with your breath. It is like trying to drain the earth of its water with a pump. It is like trying to fight demonic spirits with physical strength. These efforts are futile regardless how many times we try. This posture of not willing to partner with God is the direct result of our pride as a consequence of the fall of humanity.

Reinhold Niebuhr suggests that the fall of humanity caused a loss in our "capacity for faith, hope, and love—that is, the ability to rise above the natural order and have communion with divine and supernatural order, to know God and, in fellowship with him, to be delivered of the fears, anxieties, and sins which result from this separation from God. The fallen man is thus essentially an incomplete man, who is completed by the infusion of sacramental grace, which retires practically, though not quite, all of the supernatural virtues which were lost in the Fall."[10] He further states that man's pride is his "unwillingness to acknowledge his creatureliness. He is betrayed by his greatness to hide his weakness. He is tempted by his ability to gain his own security to deny his insecurity, and refuses to admit that he has no final security except in God. He is tempted by his knowledge to deny his ignorance. (This is the source of all "ideological taint" in human knowledge.)"[11] Therefore, it is necessary to have faith in God and be in partnership with him to achieve great things on earth.

Jesus said, "With God all things are possible" (Matt 19:26). In partnership with God we can declare in faith that nothing is too difficult for God (Jer 32:27). Moreover, when we accept God's word by faith and "believe that He is, and that He is a rewarder of those who diligently seek Him" (Heb 11:6), we can be victorious over any situation. Notice I keep using the word *faith*, "for without faith, it is impossible to please God" (Heb 11:6). Faithlessness is fatal to our efforts. It is like trying to drive a car with no oil or gas. It is like walking over broken glass hoping to receive no cuts and bruises. Faithlessness kept the children of Israel from reaching the promised land, and it will keep us from achieving our goals and coming into our destiny. Faith is necessary, and putting faith in action is imperative if we expect God's power to give us supernatural results. There is no way Moses's strength alone could have delivered the children of Israel. But Moses's faith in God—and his decision to act on his faith—ended the long night of oppression for many of God's children. The opening of the Red Sea was an act of faith and the power of God.

Consequently, faith is the TNT—the standard measure of strength of bombs and other explosives—in us. It is the atomic bomb of accomplishments that could explode, which could transform the world around us. Faith then is not optional; it is mandatory. Without TNT there can be no major explosions of accomplishments through us. Faith in God rests on the foundational belief that there is no power that can surpass the power of God. There is none like God in heaven, in earth, nor beneath the earth. There is no power anywhere in the visible or invisible world that equals God. Isaiah said,

> Who has measured the waters in the hollow of his hand, or with the breadth of his hand marked off the heavens? Who has held the dust of the earth in a basket, or weighed the mountains on the scales and the hills in a balance?... Surely the nations are like a drop in a bucket; they are regarded as dust on the scales; he weighs the islands as though they were fine dust.... Before him all the nations are as nothing; they are regarded by him as worthless and less than nothing. With whom, then, will you compare God? (Isa 40:12–18)

This is the God we must have faith in—the God of Jesus Christ, who raised him from the dead. Faith in anything else—money, position, power—won't yield supernatural results. Many people have put their faith in the idol gods of this world only to be disappointed, betrayed, and destroyed. Like the prophets of Baal who called upon him and were never answered, so it is with us who put faith in idol gods. Therefore, for God to accomplish amazing things through us, we must have faith in the true and living God and be willing risk-takers, doers, and people of action. Although at times we may not know the outcome of our actions, we still must act by faith, believing God, who declared, "I make known the end from the beginning, from ancient times, what is still to come" (Isa 46:10). One thing is certain: God will not leave us in shame or allow our efforts to do his will be defeated. We must walk by faith, not by sight (2 Cor 5:7).

What is faith? According to the scripture, "faith is the substance of things hoped for, the evidence of things not seen" (Heb 11:1). Faith doesn't mean all the details will be disclosed. It doesn't mean seeing before believing. Faith is stepping into the unknown and trusting God despite the circumstances. It means holding on to God's word when the situation and circumstances dictate letting go. It means echoing with conviction, "Though he slay me, yet will I hope in him" (Job 13:15).

When we trust God in the deep darkness without wavering, God accomplishes great things in and through us. When Shadrach, Meshach, and Abednego faced imminent death in a fiery furnace for not bowing to an idol god, faith stood and spoke: "King Nebuchad-nezzar, we do not need to defend ourselves before you in this matter. If we are thrown into the blazing furnace, the God we serve is able to deliver us from it, and he will deliver us from Your Majesty's hand. But even if he does not, we want you to know, Your Majesty, that we will not serve your gods or worship the image of gold you have set up" (Dan 3:16–18). God delivered them, and the king was convinced that God is God.

However, it is not enough simply to communicate faith; we must be willing to demonstrate it, "for faith without works is dead" (Jas 2:20). God is willing to demonstrate and orchestrate his power through us when we live and act by faith. Every place where God has shown himself strong came through those willing to act on faith. They were not the smartest, not the most promising, not the most moral, not the most qualified. Yet they acted on their faith in God, who looked beyond their problems and saw their potential. Their faith moved God to perform some wonderful miracles through them. The same can happen for us because "God shows no partiality." (Acts 10:34).

Equally, God is willing to use ordinary, untrained, unqualified, and deeply flawed people who are willing to act on faith to achieve some amazing things. Acts 4:13 says, "When they saw the courage of Peter and John and realized that they were unschooled, ordinary men, they were astonished and they took note that these men had been with Jesus." Many people may question people's usefulness to God because they are poor, uneducated, unknown, unimportant. Some may feel that their background of lawlessness or criminal behavior disqualifies them from being used by God. Others may feel that since they have not come from a line of preachers, scholars, educators, protestors, they are the last people God would think about using. Some may feel that their age is a factor of God not using them for someone much younger or someone much older. All of these reasons are invalid because biblical and contemporary history show that God uses people across ethnic, color, class, gender, age, religious, and political lines. Whomever God wants to use, God qualifies. Whomever God wants to promote, God picks. And God's selection sometimes comes from the most unpromising soil.

The main point is not the perfection of a person, though Jesus wants us to strive for it, but having faith in God and putting this faith in action. Faith is like traveling through the fog even if you cannot see the path. It is like throwing your fishing line in the water though you do not see the fish. It is like going up the stairs though you don't see the whole staircase. It is like sitting down on a chair believing it will hold you up. God wants us to have this kind of faith and confidence in him. Regardless of the situation and circumstances, God will perform his good will and purpose through us when we put faith in action. To transform the world around us takes partnership with God and operating in faith. The problems in our world—oppression, racism, sexism, terrorism, injustice, war, police brutality, etc.—are not greater than God. They can be solved by faith. God and humanity working together can transform dark yesterdays into bright tomorrows.

Scripture says "by faith" Abel, Enoch, Noah, Abraham, Sarah, Isaac, Moses, etc. (Heb 11:1–8). These people all acted by faith despite their imperfections and limitations in the world. Faith, then, "is an essential possibility of man, and therefore its existence is necessary and universal. It is possible and necessary also in our period. If faith is understood as what it centrally is, ultimate concern, it cannot be undercut by modern science or any kind of philosophy. And it cannot be discredited by its superstitions or authoritarians distortions within and outside churches, sects and movements."[12] For God through Christ to use us in these last days, to transform our broken and lost world, we must act by faith so our names will be added to the roll of the faithful. The roll of the faithful was a vast group of people. Many were poor, untrained, immoral, and uneducated. A few were rich, some were crooks, and others were social outcasts. God is willing to transform and use anyone to do his will, regardless of what they do or do not possess: "The just shall live by faith" (Rom 1:17). Regardless of what is going on in and around us, we must keep our relationship with God fresh and thriving. In the final consummation, the faithful are justified through Jesus Christ our Lord.

Therefore, "faith is the one condition on which all Divine power can enter into man and work through him. It is the susceptibility of the unseen: man's will yielded up to, and moulded by, the will of God."[13] Those whom God uses to carry out his will and good purpose are all arrested by God's power and transformed by God's love, grace, and mercy. Heaven's book is still adding names of people who lived in faith, acted by faith, received in faith, and experienced God's transforming power by faith. What about your name? This book is written to help you live in and act on your faith in God through Jesus Christ.

Whatever God says, we must hear and obey. It is through hearing the word of God that faith is awakened in us. By acting on faith we receive the blessing through obedience: "Obedience and faith must go together. Not as if to the faith he has the obedience must be added, but faith must be made manifest in obedience. Faith is obedience at home and looking to the Master: obedience is faith going out to do His will."[14] The same God who lived in and worked through the faithful is willing to do the same through us.

Chapter one of this book focuses on having faith in God. Chapter two focuses on growing in the faith. Chapter three focuses on the Kingdom of God not as talk but action. It is not a matter of profession but power. Power to arrest the dark forces of life that are often a nightmare and unending holocaust. Chapter four focuses on faith in action. Chapter five focuses on bold faith. Chapter six focuses on faith and politics. Chapter seven focuses on remaining faithful. It is my hope and prayer that this book will deepen your faith, motivate you to live by and act on faith to transform the world around you, and strengthen your resolve to remain faithful that you may be the recipient of the promises of God through Jesus Christ in this world and the one to come.

ENDNOTES

[1] Robert P. Vande Kappelle and John D. Currie, "The Old Testament: The Covenant Between God and Man," *Building a Christian Worldview*, ed. W. Andrew Hoffecker and Gary Scott Smith (Phillipsburg NJ: Presbyterian and Reformed Publishing Company, 1986), 25.

[2] Walter Rauschenbusch, "The Workers," *Walter Rauschenbusch: Selected Writings*, Sources of American Spirituality, ed. Winthrop S. Hudson (Mahwah NJ: Paulist Press, 1984), 100.

[3] Curl Oral Hazell, *Real Faith in Action: The Demonstration of Nine Principles that Characterize Authentic Faith* (Eugene OR: Wipf & Stock Publishers, 2009), 18–19.

[4] Martin Buber, *Hasidism* (New York: Philosophical Library, 1948), 108–109.

[5] Harvey Cox, *The Secular City* (New York: The Macmillan Co., 1968), 231–32.

[6] Karl Barth, The Christian Life The Gracious God as the Commanding God," *Church Dogmatics*, vol. 4.4 (Grand Rapids: William B. Eerdmans Publishing Company, 1981), 29.

[7] Ibid., 43.

[8] A. W. Tozer, *Paths to Power: Living in the Spirit's Fullness* (Chicago: Moody Bible Institute, 1940), 24.

[9] Martin Luther King Jr., *Strength to Love* (Philadelphia: Fortress Press, 1963), 112.

[10] Reinhold Niebuhr, "Christian Faith and Natural Law," *Christian Social Teaching*, compiled and edited by George W. Forell (Minneapolis: Augsburg Publishing House, 1966), 394.

[11] Ibid., 395.

[12] Paul Tillich, *Dynamics of Faith* (New York: Harper & Row, 1957), 126.

[13] Andrew Murray, *With Christ in the School of Prayer* (Virginia Beach: CBN University Press, 1978), 95.

[14] Ibid., 155.

CHAPTER ONE

HAVE FAITH IN GOD

To trust God in the light is nothing, but trust him in the dark
—that is faith.

—C. H. Spurgeon

To have faith in God is to have total trust and confidence in God that God will never leave nor forsake us. It means allowing God to work in and through us to achieve God's good will and purpose. Faith in God is to relinquish all outcomes to God while participating in the process with God. Paul Tillich said, "There is no faith without participation!"[1] Therefore, in the process of participation, we may not see God's hand, but we must trust God's heart; we may not understand God's design, but we must trust God's plan. Regardless of life's circumstances, faith in God is trust and confidence in him at all times. Against all odds, against all rationality, against all evidence, and against the vicissitudes of life, faith in God is to stand on his word and to believe that what God says will come to pass. This is what Paul Tillich calls the "ultimate concern" of faith. Our ultimate concern is to have faith in God, who "magnifies [his] word above all [his] name" (Ps 138:2), and that God's word "shall accomplish what [God] pleases, and it shall prosper in the thing for which [God] sent it" (Isa 55:11). In other words, whatever God says, that settles it: "The Lord is not lack concerning His promise, as some count slackness" (2 Pet 3:9). God will perform his word in and through faith! A. W. Tozer says, "True faith rests upon the character of God and asks no further proof than the moral perfections of the One who cannot lie. It is enough that God said it, and if the statement should contradict every one of the five senses and all the conclusions of logic as well, still the believer continues to believe. 'Let God be true, but every man a liar,' is the language of true faith. Heaven approves such faith because it rises above mere proofs and rests in the bosom of God."[2]

When God told Noah to build an ark before the flood, Noah had faith in God to believe that what God said would come to pass. Without wavering in his faith, Noah got busy building the ark at God's instruction. Although there was no rain cloud in sight and no evidence to prove it was going to rain—and against the scoffing and unbelief of the people—Noah went about building the ark. Noah's faith in God kept him working and trusting that a great deluge would eventually come because God said it would. "Since faith leads to action,"[3] Noah took action and saved himself, his family, and the animals that came aboard in the ark. Noah's ultimate concern was the preservation of community. The community refused to join him in the faith; therefore, the community lost their lives in the great flood. Noah put his faith in God while the people put faith in themselves. Having faith in God doesn't mean others will join us in the faith. But regardless of others, we should always put faith in God and obey him at all cost. When we obey God, it is the consequence of faith: "The man that believes will obey; failure to obey is convincing proof that there is not true faith present. To attempt the impossible, God must give faith or there will be none, and He gives faith to the obedient heart only."[4]

Another example of faith in God is the life of Abraham. Since Abraham is called the friend of God, his life is a prime example of not only having faith in God, but putting this faith in action. When God told Abraham to leave his country, his kindred, and his father's house, Abraham had enough faith in God to take the risk (Gen 12:1–4). Faith is risk-taking. It is Søren Kierkegaard's "Leap of Faith," which means leaping into the unknown, the unseen, and the unproved, while having faith in God, who is reliable and trustworthy. The promise made to Abraham through faith was fulfilled. The fulfillment of the promise took time, and Abraham made mistakes, and we too will make mistakes in the process. But God is faithful despite our mistakes. Abraham's mistake was taking into consideration his old age. But God wants us to have faith despite our age and circumstances. The promise to Abraham was fulfilled because Abraham totally trusted God. We cannot totally trust God until we have a solid relationship with God. When our relationship with God is sound, then it is easy to accept the promise of God with it.

After some time God blessed Abraham with Isaac, and then God asked Abraham to sacrifice Isaac unto him. Because of Abraham's deep and abiding faith in God, it was no problem to give back to God what was given to him by faith. Abraham took his son and put him on the altar to sacrifice unto the Lord. The faith connection of Abraham to God left no doubt in Abraham's heart that somehow he would return home with Isaac. Before going up to the place to sacrifice Isaac, Abraham told his servants, "Stay here with the donkey while I and the boy go over there. We will worship and then we will come back to you" (Gen 22:5). Notice Abraham said, "*We* will come back to you." Deep within the recesses of Abraham's heart, his faith in God was such that his ultimate concern was not Isaac's death, but obeying his omnipotent God. Abraham passed the test of faith. He did not have to sacrifice Isaac, and God "credited it to him as righteousness" (Gen 15:6) because his faith in God was based upon an abiding relationship with God, which led to obedience to God. The lesson is this: "We seek God's gifts: God wants to give us Himself first. We think of prayer as the power to draw down good gifts from heaven; Jesus as the means to draw ourselves up to God. We want to stand at the door and cry; Jesus would have us first enter in and realize that we are friends and children.... Let every experience of the littleness of our faith...urge us first to have and exercise more faith in the living God, and in such faith to yield ourselves to Him."[5]

God wants us first to want him above everything. Too many people pray to God for blessings without intending to obey and without desiring a relationship with God. When people are blessed, they get caught up in the blessings and forget the one who is the source of the blessings. People want the promises, not the Provider; they want the gifts, not the Giver; they want the blessings, not the Blesser. For this reason God told the children of Israel, "When you eat and are satisfied, when you build fine houses and settle down, and when your herds and flocks grow large and your silver and gold increase and all you have is multiplied, then your heart will become proud and you will forget the LORD your God, who brought you out of Egypt, out of the land of slavery" (Deut 8:12–14). The danger of blessings is that we put our faith in our wisdom, our technology, our military, our possessions, our system, not in God. No wonder there is a great falling away from the faith; people are looking for resources, not a relationship with God through Jesus Christ.

To have faith in God is to "seek first the kingdom of God and His righteousness; and all these things shall be added to you" (Matt 6:33). God wants us to first put his will above everything else in the world. Faith is first rooted in relationship with God. Andrew Murray states,

> Have faith in God, the living God: let faith look to God more than the thing promised: it is love, His power, His living presence will waken and work the faith.... Learn to believe in God, to take hold of God, to let God take possession of thy life, and it will be easy to take hold of the promise. He that knows and trusts God finds it easy to trust the promise too.... Therefore, have faith in God: let faith be all eye and ear, the surrender to let God make His full impression, and reveal Himself fully in the soul. Count it one of the chief blessings of prayer to exercise faith in God, as the Living Mighty God who waits to fulfill in us all the good pleasure of His will, and the work of faith with power.[6]

Jesus, our quintessential example, knew what it would take to make this time-bound journey of life. He knew that life would be a process of challenges that would sometimes cloud our sight, making it difficult for us to see where we are going. Jesus is very much aware of what our needs are on life's journey. Having faith in God through our relationship with him, Jesus said, "Your Father knows what you need before you ask him" (Matt 6:8).

Abraham H. Maslow identified five basic human needs on life's journey. He stated that these needs are common to all humans, regardless of language and culture. Maslow talked about needs such as physiological needs, safety needs, love needs, esteem needs, and self-actualization needs. Maslow believed that if a basic need is left unsatisfied, the result is generally a psychological sickness. Though we may agree with Maslow about basic human needs, Jesus takes it a step further by reminding us that among the many things we need on our life's journey—such as love, food, water, education, money, fellowship, and other sustenance—we also need something else; we need a consistent, abiding faith in God, because "man cannot live by bread alone, but by every word that proceeds out of the mouth of God" (Matt 4:4).

We may be deprived of one or more of Maslow's basic human needs, but we must never allow this deprivation to cause us to lose faith in God. Jesus wants us to understand that God is our sustainer and keeper: "The birds of the air neither sow nor reap nor gather into barns, yet [our] heavenly Father feeds them. Are [we] not of more value than they?... But if God so clothes the grass of the field...will He not much more clothe [us]?" (Matt 6:26, 30). Jesus is saying to us through the annals of time, "Have faith in God." God knows your needs. Jesus encourages us to make God our total trust above anything in the world. God knows how to take care of our needs. As food and water are necessary for this life's journey, faith in God is also necessary for the journey. Faith is the only means by which we can receive the promises of God. We may not see the harvest of the seed we plant, but faith motivates us to plant anyhow. We may not see the seed of values we plant in our children and the next generation, but faith moves us to plant anyhow. Joseph did not see the enslavement of his people in Egypt but he had faith that God would visit and lead them to the

Promised Land. Faith moved Joseph to order the Israelites to take his bones with them during their departure. Walter Rauschenbush stated,

> In sowing the truth a man may never see or trace the results. The more ideal his conceptions are, and the farther they move ahead of his time, the larger will be the percentage of apparent failure. But he can afford to wait. The powers of life are on his side. He is like a man who has scattered his seed and then goes off to sleep by night and work by day, and all the while the seed, by the inscrutable chemistry of life, lays hold of the ingredients of its environment and builds them up to its own growth. The mustard-seed becomes a tree. The leaven assimilates the meal by biological processes. The new life penetrates the old humanity and transforms it.[7]

We may not see the end results of our moral struggles, but if we plant the seed of morality, justice, and righteousness by faith, the manifestation will eventually be made known. Martin Luther King Jr. stated in his last speech, "I may not get there with you but I want you to know tonight that we as a people will get to the Promised Land."[8] King's faith in justice and righteousness went beyond his physical life, and although the oppressed were in the process of liberation, King's faith in God moved him to believe that the oppressed would get to the promised land even if their leaders were no longer with them physically. So as we do God's work, our faith in God must go beyond our physical lives. If we don't see the results of our struggles while we are living, we must maintain faith in God that the next generation will. Whatever we are struggling for in life, we must maintain faith in God that the promise will be fulfilled.

Jesus wants us to understand that we cannot walk this Christian journey without faith. We cannot struggle against oppression, evil, and injustice without a working faith in God. When our best efforts fail, we need faith in God to help us try again. It doesn't matter how much we come to church, how much we march against structural injustice and institutional racism and those things that make life a nightmare and an unending holocaust; without faith, we bear no fruit. This should convince us that faith is all-important, and as Christians we must not only have faith in God but demonstrate faith in our daily lives. If we never bring faith to bear upon our divided and torn world, how can we lead others to the faith? How can we ever convince the world that there is a "balm in Gilead that can heal the sin-sick soul and make the wounded whole"[9] unless we walk, live, and struggle by faith and not by sight? By faith our actions in this world give people a glimpse of God that they would not otherwise have:

> Faith as the Bible knows it is confidence in God and His Son Jesus Christ; it is the response of the soul to the divine character as revealed in the scriptures; and even this response is impossible apart from the prior in working of the Holy Spirit. Faith is a gift of God to a penitent soul and has nothing whatsoever to do with the senses or the data they afford. Faith is a miracle; it is the ability God gives to trust His Son, and anything that does not result in action in accord with the will of God is not faith but something else short of it.[10]

Every person in the world exercises faith in something, though it may fall short of the faith God gives: "One does not eat his dinner or lie down on his bed at night without faith that the food will nourish and not poison him, that the bed will support and not suffocate him. One does not usually go to the doctor unless he has faith that the doctor will help him get well. One does not or ought not to marry without faith that the other person will cooperate to form a home."[11] Some people have faith in their jobs, in their money, in their degrees, in the government, in their social status and sociopolitical position. These things are known to fail people at one time or another; they are not reliable. Family members, friends, neighbors, churches, government systems, and leaders will let us down in life. They may not intend to, but they are human; they are limited. Scripture teaches us not to "put your trust in princes, in human beings, who cannot save. When their spirit departs, they return to the ground; on that very day their plans come to nothing. Blessed are those whose help is the God of Jacob, whose hope is in the LORD their God" (Ps 146:3–5). Jesus wants us to put our faith in God, who is limitless and who will never fail nor forsake us.

Faith in God "is the union of trusting confidence and courageous action with response to God's leading, and of all these with the insight that lights the way toward truth. It is this combination that makes Christian faith such a powerful force."[12] We need more active faith to help save the world from itself. Putting our faith in action while having faith in God can give us victory after victory. Of course, this doesn't mean victory will come overnight. Abraham did not receive the promised child overnight; the children of Israel did not leave Egypt overnight; Joshua did not enter the promised land overnight; Nehemiah did not build a wall around Jerusalem overnight. All of these events took time, with an abiding faith in God that eventually the victory would be won. Having faith in God means to wait while we work: "No one knows what the future holds. Most of the time, God's plan is beyond our grasp and often beyond even the reach of our imagination."[13] When God reveals his word and purpose to us, we should never doubt him, even though we cannot figure out how something is going to happen. It may take weeks, months, or years, but be assured that what God says will come to pass.

One of the greatest obstacles that gets in the way of our faith in God is our reasoning. We try to figure out how God is going to do something when we ought to just trust God to do what he said he would. There are numerous examples of men and women who not only believed in God but who demonstrated a responsive faith in the word of God. They didn't try to figure out how God was going to do what he said; they simply trusted God. They believed in the unrivaled authority, decisive importance, immense power, and complete reliability of God's word: "By faith, Noah, being warned by God concerning events as yet unseen, took heed and constructed an ark for the saving of his household.... By faith Abraham obeyed when he was called to go out to a place which he was to receive as an inheritance; and he went out, not knowing where he was to go.... For he looked for a city...whose builder and maker is God. By faith Sarah herself received power to conceive, even when she was past the age, since she considered him faithful who had promised" (Heb 11:8–11). Throughout Scripture there are numerous of examples of people who put their faith in the one who is faithful and who cannot lie. Those with faith in God accept God's word, win God's approval, and witness God's power.

Many people are defeated and destroyed because they have no knowledge of the Word of God, and there is no way one's faith can grow without the knowledge of God's Word. Scripture tells us that "faith comes by hearing, and hearing by the Word of God.... And how shall they hear without a preacher?" (Rom 10:14, 17; order reversed). It is a sad fact that many people come to a church meeting but stay home or have other obligations on Bible study night and Sunday school hour, when the Word of God is being taught. Have you often wondered why people continue to act the way they do in church, at home, or in the community? It is the result of not having the Word of God in them that is necessary for growth. Like water and sunlight are necessary for plant life to grow, the Word of God is necessary for God's people to grow. Many people who attend church can tell you about their denomination, their bylaws, their rules and regulations, but still have no knowledge and understanding about spiritual matters. We cannot respond in faith to what we do not believe in knowledge. The Spirit won't give what the mind rejects. Some people hear the Word of God and reject it because they say or think it does not make sense. Sometimes it does not make sense; it makes faith, and faith in God cannot rest on our senses or the flimsy evaluation and calculation of our finite minds. Faith must rest on what God says, and if God said it, regardless of how nonsensical it might seem, that should settle it. When God said we are free and free indeed, that should settle it (John 8:36). When God says we shall walk through the fire and not be burned and go through the deep waters and not drown, that should settle it (Isa 43:2). Much of what God says does not appeal to our natural senses; it appeals to our faith.

I don't want to give you the impression that faith is a blindfolded leap into the dark of the unknown. Faith is based upon knowledge; it is not a substitute for knowledge. As our knowledge grows, our faith grows. What knowledge, you may ask? Is it academic? Scientific? Political and economic? No. The knowledge I am referring to where faith is concerned is the knowledge of the Word of God. God said, "My people are destroyed for a lack of knowledge" (Hos 4:6). They are destroyed not because they are educated in the great halls of learning, not because they don't possess a high IQ, but because they have a lack of knowledge of the Word of God. And if they know the Word of God, it is only head knowledge, not heart knowledge. In order words, they intellectualize it and rationalize it but won't obey it, which is an indicator that they don't really believe it. Many have dismissed it as myth and therefore refuse to obey it. Remember how Saul, the first king of Israel, constantly disobeyed God's commandments and eventually lost his throne? When we don't obey the Word of God by rationalizing to do things our way, we end up miserable, bitter, angry, defeated, and destroyed. Some people never advance spiritually "in the vanity of their mind, having their understanding darkened, being alienated from the life of God through the ignorance that is in them, because of the blindness of their heart" (Eph 4:18).

Jesus does not want us to walk in spiritual blindness, but to have faith in God. He knows the Christian journey includes mountains of problems, valleys of despair, hills of frustration, and situations and circumstances that seem insurmountable, but faith in God gives us the power to overcome these things. Regardless of how dark it gets, faith in God serves as a lightning rod to see us through the gloom. Never stop having faith in God, because when life storms eclipse our way, faith gets us through. When the haze of frustration blocks our view, keep faith in God, because the haze won't last. I once read a story about a helicopter pilot who flew through a storm over the

Pacific Ocean. Though blinded by the fog, faith got him through it. The story goes like this:

> I was flying the helicopter back to the ship when a blinding fog rolled in. Flying at a low altitude, I knew that a single mistake would plunge my crew and me into the ocean. Worse yet, I was experiencing a complete loss of balance—which is common for pilots flying by instruments. This loss of balance—known as vertigo was so bad that despite the instrument readings I was certain that I was lying on my side. For 15 minutes I flew the helicopter by its instruments, fighting the urge to turn it according to my feelings. When we finally broke safely through the fog, I was deeply thankful I had been trained to rely upon my instruments rather than on my feelings.[14]

This is what people of faith must do—trust God and not feelings. Feelings are fickle; feeling can be misleading. But the Word of God is reliable, trustworthy, and consistent. When we are going through the fog of misunderstanding, persecution, scarcity, or loneliness, we must rely on the instrument of God's Word. Faith in God sees us through the thick fog of life. It gives us the strength and split moments of transcendence to overcome every adversity:

> It is faith to assume that this is a good world and that life is worth living. It is faith to assert the feasibility of a fairly righteous and fraternal social order. In the midst of a despotic and predatory industrial life it is faith to stake our business future on the proposition that fairness, kindness, and fraternity will work. When war inflames a nation, it is faith to believe that a peaceable disposition is a workable international policy. Amidst the disunion of Christendom it is faith to look for unity and to express unity in action. It is faith to see God at work in the world and to claim a share in his job. Faith is an energetic act of will, affirming our fellowship with God and

man, declaring our solidarity with the Kingdom of God, and repudiating selfish isolation.[15]

When we bring faith to bear on life situations, we may not get immediate results but ripples of hope not to give up on the possibility of transformation.

ENDNOTES

[1] Paul Tillich, *Dynamics of Faith* (New York: Harper & Row, 1957), 100.

[2] A. W. Tozer, *Man: The Dwelling Place of God* (San Francisco: Fig Publisher, 2012), 23.

[3] Tillich, *Dynamics of Faith*, 117.

[4] Tozer, *Man: The Dwelling Place of God*, 24.

[5] Andrew Murray, *With Christ in the School of Prayer* (Virginia Beach: CBN University Press, 1978), 92.

[6] Ibid., 90–92.

[7] Walter Rauschenbusch, "A Public Ministry: 'Christianity And The Social Crisis,'" *Walter Rauschenbusch: Selected Writings*, Sources of American Spirituality, ed. Winthrop S. Hudson (Mahwah NJ: Paulist Press, 1984), 162.

[8] Martin Luther King Jr., "I've Been to the Mountaintop," speech, Mason Temple (Church of God in Christ), Memphis, Tennessee, April 3, 1968.

[9] Negro Spiritual, arr. by Nolan Williams Jr., b. 1969, 2000, GIA Publications, Inc.

[10] Tozer, *Man: The Dwelling Place of God*, 24.

[11] Georgia Harkness, *Understanding the Christian Faith* (Nashville: Abingdon-Cokesbury Press, 1947), 18–19.

[12] Ibid., 23.

[13] Nick Vujicic, *Unstoppable: The Incredible Power of Faith in Action* (New York: WaterBrook Press, 2012), 17.

[14] Benjamin Speare-Hardy II, "You of Little Faith, Why Did You Doubt?," sermon, Saint Margaret's Episcopal Church, Trotwood, Ohio, August 10, 2008.

[15] Rauschenbusch, "A Public Ministry: 'The Social Gospel and Personal Salvation,'" 201–202.

CHAPTER TWO

GROWING IN FAITH

Your faith will grow not by chance but by choice
—Neil L. Andersen

With the right nutrients, the right environment, and the right nurturing, babies are expected to grow. Of course, there are babies born with physical challenges that prevent their normal physical growth, but such limitations do not prevent their ability to grow psychologically, emotionally, and spiritually to bring glory to God. For example, Nick Vujicic, an internationally known personality who speaks to millions around the world, was born without arms and legs, yet his physical disability has blessed him in ways that he would not otherwise be blessed had he been born with arms and legs. Physical disability is no bar against glorifying God:

> The purpose of a child born without arms or legs was a mystery revealed slowly as I grew in faith. As I've noted before, one of the keys for me was reading in John 9:3 about the man born blind. Jesus performs a miracle to heal him and explains that His purpose for this man was to use to display God's glory. This scripture helped me realized that God might also have a purpose for me. Maybe, like the man born without sight, I'd been created without arms and legs so that God could deliver a message or somehow work through me.[1]

Just like we are expected to grow physically as babies, we are also expected to grow spiritually when we accept Jesus Christ as our Lord and Savior. As believers in Jesus Christ, we are now planted in the soil of God's grace and mercy. Therefore, spiritual growth is our responsibility. It is first the responsibility of the parents to provide the right nutrients, the right environment, and the right nurturing for proper growth to happen. It is also the responsibility of parents to provide for spiritual growth in the same way. Once children reach adulthood, it is their responsibility to take ownership of their lives and continue to grow intellectually and spiritually. Spiritual growth is not an automatic phenomenon; if it were, there would be no need for Scripture to point out, "My people are destroyed for a lack of knowledge" (Hos 4:6). We must be intentional about spiritual and intellectual growth. Growth is not by chance but by choice. Frederick Douglass stated, "Without culture there can be no growth; without exertion, no acquisition; without friction, no polish; without labor, no knowledge; without action, no progress and without conflict, no victory. A man that lies down a fool at night, hoping that he will waken wise in the morning, will rise up in the morning as he laid down in the evening. Faith, in the absence of work, seems to be worth little, if anything."[2] It is up to us to expand our minds and do what is necessary to grow into maturity.

God has given us the tools to make of this life what we desire to be, but God is not going to do this for us. Paul Tillich says, "Man creates what he is. Nothing is given to him to determine his creativity. The essence of his being—the 'should-be,' 'the ought-to-be,'—is not something which he finds; he makes it. Man is what he makes of himself. And the courage to be as oneself is the courage to make of oneself what one wants to be."[3] Character building is our responsibility; attitude adjustment is our responsibility; humbling ourselves and submitting to the lordship of Jesus Christ is our responsibility. God cannot do this for us. To wait on God to do for us what we can do for ourselves is not faith but superstition. We must do what is commanded of us by God, and when we fail to do our part, we cannot expect to be given certain tasks when we lack the maturity.

A major problem in our world, especially in America, is that people have grown physically, but they are still babies spiritually.

There are many people who go to the gym and exercise to stay fit physically but won't go to church or a Bible study to grow spiritually. These are people who say they have accepted Jesus Christ as Lord. Now, there is nothing wrong with going to the gym, but to be disciples of Jesus Christ, we must be students of the scriptures to get fit and stay fit spiritually. Just like we exercise physically, we must exercise spiritually to grow in faith. We must never forget that we are in a spiritual warfare, and to transform the world as Jesus did requires spiritual fitness. Many have privileges, power, and access but are not spiritually strong enough to resist the enemy of their souls, who is constantly trying to destroy them. This is not to convey that the poor, the underprivileged, and those who have no access are any different. The same enemy after the rich is also after the poor. The same enemy after democracy is the same enemy after other forms of government. To fight and overcome our common enemy requires spiritual growth. To gain spiritual growth requires the consistent study of the Word of God: "The Word of God is rich beyond comprehension to supply hope for literally every situation in our lives. The devil, because he is aware of this, utilizes his influence on the world and our flesh in making every attempt to keep us from reading it. When we do not read it, however, we actually give the Holy Spirit very little to work with in being able to illuminate that word to our hearts that we might embrace it by faith to achieve results."[4]

Peter, an apostle of Jesus Christ, encouraged those who accepted the Christian faith to grow in the Lord. Christian growth is not optional; it is not a suggestion or a good idea but a command. Every Christian should grow to be fruitful for the kingdom of God, and if we don't grow and bear fruit, Jesus said, "My Father…cuts off every branch in me that bears no fruit" (John 15:2). It is dangerous for a Christian not to grow and bear fruit because that Christian could be cut off by God. We could lose not only fellowship with God but lose our souls as well. When a plant doesn't receive proper water, sunlight, and attention, it could die even though the soil in which it is planted is healthy. So it is with Christian growth. If we have planted our faith in the soil of God's grace and mercy, God expects us to grow so we can be used to do the will of God on earth and reach others to advance the kingdom of God. Therefore, if we expect to transform America, overturn unjust policies, get rid of racial and political divisions, correct the criminal justice system, close the income gap of inequality, and make justice an organic law of this land, it is going to take a level of spiritual maturity to achieve these things. Yes, this is a tall order indeed, but with determination and spiritual maturity we can achieve it if we believe it. Our nation and the world are in need of principled Christians who are wise, humane, just, and spiritually mature.

To grow into mature Christians, the apostle Peter told the early Christians not to stop at the point of receiving Christ through faith; rather, they needed to continue to grow in the faith and mature as new creatures in Christ: "The Christian life must not be an initial spasm followed by a chronic inertia."[5] Conversion should not be a good feeling and a moment of enthusiasm that then peters out and dwindles to nothing. A Christian life must always thrive to grow and mature in the Lord. A tree that never matures never bears fruit, and if we are not bearing fruit, it is due to our neglect to do what is necessary to grow in the soil of God's grace. Growth is our responsibility. God has given us the grace, the tools, and the opportunity, but it is our responsibility to take what has been provided and grow in the faith. God has given us the ground, the seed, and the rain, but it is the responsibility of every farmer to till the soil, sow the seed, get rid of the weeds and the parasites, and do other necessary things in order to have a great harvest. The Christian life is no different. We must do our part and till the soil of our minds, sow the seed of goodness, get rid of the weeds of doubt and the parasites of bad company so our lives can have a great harvest. God will not do for us what we can do for ourselves. God has given us his Word, his grace, and his Spirit, but it is our responsibility to grow and mature in our faith.

How are we to grow spiritually when we never read and meditate upon the Word of God? Has entertainment, such as television, video, and handheld devices, taken away our desire to read? Have we allowed materialism and technological advancements to overshadow the nurturing of the soul? If so, this explains the ever-increasing decadence of society and the forsaking of many Christians to assemble themselves together to receive spiritual teaching and nurturing. Curl Oral Hazell made this cogent observation:

> In our present visual, entertainment society, by and large, we have become disinterested in reading on a whole. Tragically, this disinterest has trickled down to include the believer's approach to the word of God, which leads to our over dependence on others to read and study the word for us. This attitude signifies irresponsibility not only with matters pertaining to this life but also those of eternity. When we do not read the word for ourselves we make ourselves easy prey to false teachings that result from others' uninformed interpretations or their willful use of the word to manipulate others. Regardless of the reason for their error, the effects can be destructive. On the one hand, we can develop a false hope in which to put our trust, while on the other hand, we may be deprived of knowing the truth of the word so that we can believe it.[6]

Therefore, if we are misled by others due to our refusal to make time to study God's Word for our spiritual growth, we have no one to blame but ourselves.

Every Christian must understand that even Jesus grew in wisdom and stature (see Luke 2:52). Jesus studied the scriptures (for moral and spiritual wisdom), which gave him favor with God; he also grew in stature (physically) and socially (favor with men). Now, if we are to be like Jesus, we must grow in all these areas as well. Although Jesus is the Son of God, he took it upon himself to grow his faith and not leave his growth to someone else. People may say that Jesus was God. The existential question is can God grow? Is God limited? The point here is that Jesus was a human being; God was working in Christ as God desires to work in us. As Jesus Christ did his part and grew his faith as a human, we must do our part and grow our faith as well. Just because the spirit of God is in us does not release us from doing our part to grow as Jesus grew. Jesus was our example par excellent, and if we are to heal this broken and torn world, we must not put our responsibility on someone else for our spiritual growth and advancement.

Another example of spiritual growth is the life of the apostle Paul. Paul said, "When I was a child I spoke as a child; I understood as a child, I thought as a child; but when I became a man, I put away childish things" (1 Cor 13:11). Paul did not remain childish in his thinking, talk, character, and lifestyle. He grew up and matured and became an outstanding soldier for Jesus Christ. He could not have written most of the New Testament books for our teaching and edification had he remained an immature, ignorant Christian. Therefore, Paul challenges Christians to overcome childish ways so they can be used by God through Christ to help our world chart a different course. Paul advised young Timothy about maturing through the study of God's Word: "Study and do your best to present yourself to God approved, a workman [tested by trial] who has no reason to be ashamed, accurately handling and skillfully teaching the word of truth" (2 Tim 2:15). To be fruitful and productive for the kingdom of God, God's people must overcome spiritual childishness. R. T. Kendall states,

> A child is the most selfish person that ever was. As far as he is concerned, the whole world revolves around him. He thinks only of himself and wants immediate gratification. He wants to be loved, but never crosses his mind to be loving. And some of us, who have been Christians for quite some time, have never moved beyond wanting to be loved, pampered, and encouraged. When will we take responsibility and begin to grow up? If we are still waiting for others to show if they care about us, we need to start caring instead.... So immaturity in Christians is just like the painless pursuit

of childhood, characterized by baby talk, selfishness, and shallowness.[7]

In the same vein listen to what God told Joshua in order for him to grow in the faith, prosper, and succeed: "Be careful to obey all the law my servant Moses gave you; do not turn from it to the right or to the left, that you may be successful wherever you go. Keep this Book of the Law always on your lips; meditate on it day and night, so that you may be careful to do everything written it. Then you will be prosperous and successful" (Josh 1:7–8). God was giving Joshua the formula for growth and success. Notice God didn't tell Joshua to depend on others like the priest, the levite, the scribes, or religious leaders to know the Law; Joshua was expected to know the Law for himself, to meditate upon it day and night. This is to say that Christians must study and meditate upon the Word of God for themselves. Of course we get help and wisdom from mature spiritual teachers in our pursuit to learn God's Word. Nevertheless, it is up to all Christians to study and meditate to grow. No one can give us growth; no one can give us character; no one can give us conduct; no one can give us personality; no one can give us behavior; no one can develop us into mature Christians. These are efforts we must develop for ourselves. I cannot emphasis this enough; Christian growth is our responsibility.

Once we are supplanted or taken out of the soil of this world and planted into the soil of the kingdom of God, God expects us to grow and bear fruit. Whatever soil we are planted in determines what kind of fruit we will produce. It doesn't matter what we call ourselves. It doesn't matter what our titles are, what position we hold; these things don't mean we are mature Christians. Jesus said, "You will know them by the fruits they bear" (Matt 7:16), not by what they call themselves, not by their titles, not by how long they have been attending church. In order words, we cannot produce the fruit of the Spirit—love, joy, peace, long-suffering, gentleness, goodness, faith, meekness, and temperance—when we are planted in the soil of this fallen world. We cannot grow spiritually when the roots of our souls are getting nutrients from the soil of this world. This is reason the post-modern church has lost much of its growth and power. We are trying to run the church, grow the church, and sustain the church by worldly standards, worldly methods, and worldly ideas. The church is a spiritual organism that should only get its nutrients, power, and authority from the Holy Spirit. When the church is dieting on what the world offers, are we surprised how cold, stale, and lifeless the church is becoming? Only the spirit of the Lord can enliven the church. Harry Emerson Fosdick states, "Ah, we respectable Christians! We have gone on building churches, elaborating complicated creeds, worshiping through splendid rituals, but how often the real spirit of Jesus has been somewhere else!"[8]

When the real spirit of Jesus Christ is somewhere else, could this be the reason the church has allowed itself to be run by unconverted, spiritually ignorant, and immature people who call themselves Christians but who act like spoiled little children? Many people who run the church have brought into it the same old evil, same old character, same old attitude, same old backwardness, and same old tricks and self-centeredness that they practice in the world. Religion has not made them better but provided an opportunity to assert their egoism and sanctify their meanness. Many of them act like the immature Diotrephes of the early church. John said, "I wrote to the church, but Diotrephes, who loves to be first, will not welcome us. So when I come, I will call attention to what he is doing, spreading malicious nonsense about us. Not satisfied with that, he even refuses to welcome other believers. He also stops those who want to do so and puts them out of the church. Dear friend, do not imitate what is evil but what is good" (3 John 1:9–11). Diotrephes practiced a self-centered religion, which produces egoism, racism, pride, arrogance, and narcissism of which Jesus says, "Woe to you, teachers of the law and Pharisees, you hypocrites! You shut the door of the kingdom of heaven in people's faces. You yourselves do not enter, nor will you let those enter who are try to" (Matt 23:13–14).

Spiritual immaturity in the postmodern church is so shame-ful that we cannot blame the world for looking at it askance. Look how racially, denominationally, and doctrinally divided the church is. Look how Christians bite and devour one another. Look how they destroy one another. Look how they are in competition with one another. Look at the ongoing "isms," such as racism, sexism, classism, and ageism. Instead of the church being the thermostat that sets the temperature of society, it has become the thermometer that registers the temperature of society. There are Christians who say they love God whom they have not seen but hate their brothers and sisters whom they have seen (1 John 4:20). There are Christians who talk about freedom but remain silent about justice, as if the two are mutually exclusive. There are Christians who talk about sexual immorality and never talk about structural racism and oppression. There are Chris-tians who talk against welfare for the poor and needy but never open their mouths against subsidies for the rich. There are Christians who support civil issues that are against the Word of God because they are worried about being on the wrong side of history. I would rather be on the wrong side of history and side with the Word of God than to be on the wrong side of eternity. Only mature Christians can stand on the Word of God regardless of politics, class, and social ostra-cism. Mature Christians understand that the gospel of Jesus Christ is not just concern about the souls of people, but their bodies and their social and economic conditions as well. Harry Emerson Fosdick stated, "Any church that pretends to care for the souls of people but is not interested in the slums that damn them, the city government that corrupts them, the economic order that cripples them, and inter-national relationships that, leading to peace or war, determine the spiritual destiny of innumerable souls—that kind of church, I think, would hear again the Master's withering words: 'Scribes and Pharisees, hypocrites!'"[9]

Therefore, if we desire to save our nation and the nations of the world from spiritual death, we must grow into spiritual maturity. It is not enough to have faith; we must add to our faith. Peter says,

"Add to your faith virtue, to virtue knowledge, to knowledge self-control, to self-control perseverance, to perseverance godliness, to godliness brotherly kindness, and to brotherly kindness love. For if these things are yours and abound, you will be neither barren nor unfruitful in the knowledge of our Lord Jesus Christ" (2 Pet 1:5–8). Like being on a ladder, we ought to take these steps every day to grow as Christians. These added steps to our faith are necessary; they are mandatory for us to have the spiritual maturity to do the will of God on earth as it is in heaven.

Notice the word Peter used here: *add*. When we don't study and meditate on the Word of God, we subtract from our faith. When we don't put first the kingdom of God and his righteousness, we subtract from our faith. When prayer meeting and Bible study are not a priority, we subtract from our faith. When we don't walk in the light, we subtract from our faith. When we forsake to assemble ourselves together to worship God in Spirit and in truth, we subtract from our faith. When we are afraid to stand up against wrong, evil, and injustice, we subtract from our faith. When we pursue the American dream and not the principles of the kingdom of God, we subtract from our faith. When we never move from membership to discipleship, we subtract from our faith. When we never move from being hearers to doers of the Word, we subtract from our faith. When we refuse to speak out against the prevailing perversion in our land because we are afraid of the consequences, we subtract from our faith. We must hurry up and add to our faith the moral standards and principles that Peter pointed out before it is too late. Peter's message to us is urgent.

William Booth, the British preacher who founded the Salvation Army reminds us, "The chief danger that confronts the coming century will be religion without the Holy Ghost, Christianity without Christ, forgiveness without repentance, salvation without regeneration, politics without God, heaven without hell."[10] Unless we add these moral imperatives to our faith and grow into spiritual maturity, Christ just may remove our lampstand from its place (Rev 2:5).

ENDNOTES

[1] Nick Vujicic, *Unstoppable: The Incredible Power of Faith in Action* (New York: WaterBrook Press, 2012), 194.

[2] Frederick Douglass, "Self-Made Men" (1893), *The Frederick Douglass Papers, Series One: Speeches, Debates and Interviews*, vol. 5: 1881–95, ed. John W. Blassingame and John R. McKivigan (New Haven: Yale University Press, 1992), 555.

[3] Paul Tillich, *The Courage to Be* (New Haven: Yale University Press, 1952), 150.

[4] Walter Rauschenbusch, ["Title of Selected Writing Should Go Here,"] *Walter Rauschenbusch: Selected Writings*, Sources of American Spirituality, ed. Winthrop S. Hudson (Mahwah NJ: Paulist Press, 1984), 23.

[5] William Barclay, *The Letters of James and Peter* (Louisville: John Knox Press, 2003), 345.

[6] Curl Oral Hazell, *Real Faith in Action: The Demonstration of Nine Principles that Characterize Authentic Faith* (Eugene OR: Wipf & Stock Publishers, 2009), 23.

[7] R. T. Kendall, "Put Away Childish Things," *Charisma Magazine* (June 27, 2011).

[8] Harry Emerson Fosdick, *Answers to Real Problems: Harry Emerson Fosdick Speaks to Our Time*, ed. Mark E. Yurs (Eugene OR: Wipf & Stock Publishers, 2008), 39.

[9] Harry Emerson Fosdick, *The Hope of the World* (New York: Garden City Books, 1953), 25.

[10] William Booth, cited from "1900 Figures Forecast: A Century's Danger," ABCNews, New York, December 30, 1900.

CHAPTER THREE

KINGDOM OF GOD

Not Talk, but Power

Allow us, Lord, to demonstrate our faith by what we do, so that the gospel can be seen by those who seek for You.

—Sper

Sidney W. Powell once said, "How much valuable time is wasted in meaningless chit-chat! When the telephone was invented, someone told Thoreau that now the people in Massachusetts could talk to the people in Texas. Thoreau wisely questioned, 'But suppose the people in Massachusetts have nothing to say to the people in Texas?'"[1] We are living in times of much talk. People have so much to say but accomplish so little. Never before in history has talk outrun action: "Hardly a day passes that the newspapers do not carry one or another of the headlines 'Talks to Begin' or 'Talks to Continue' or 'Talks to Resume.'"[2] People are talking on radios, television, internet, social media, and on all kinds of technical devices, but the problems of the world are still unsolved. There is talk about racism, terrorism, injustice, inequality, poverty, health care, homelessness, gun violence, etc., but little to nothing is getting done.

Could it be that talking is big business? Could it be that talking is more prosperous than actually doing something about the problems of the world? People are getting paid big bucks to talk about problems and issues. There is much talk about one nation, under God, indivisible, with liberty and justice for all, but our nation is still racially and politically divided. We have become the divided states of America. Is there really justice for all? Look at the statistics on the number of unarmed African-American men being gun down and killed by police, yet the argument is over respect for the flag and not respect for life. Look how the income gap between the rich and poor has widened. Look how health care for "the least of these" is still a point of contention in one of the richest nations in the world. Look how the church is divided and how hostility is on the rise. We are having conversations about these matters, but we are devoid of corrective actions to bring about real transformation. The reason is lip service.

> It is now quite possible to talk for hours with civilized men and women and gain absolutely nothing from it. Conversations today is almost wholly sterile. Should the talk start on a fairly high level, it is sure within a few minutes to degenerate into cheap gossip, shoptalk, banter, weak humor, stale jokes, puns and secondhand quips. So we shall omit conversations from our list of useful intellectual activities, at least until there has been a radical reformation in the art of social discourse.[3]

Tozer believes it is futile to keep conversing about issues until we are really ready to engage in actions to solve them. It seems we are more comfortable in the paralysis of analysis than in the throes of actually doing something about them. Could it be that Walter Rauschenbusch is right in saying, "No wrong can stand very long after the people have lost their reverence for it and begin to say 'Booh' to it."[4] Only when America, especially at the behest of the Christian church, loses its taste for racism, sexism, hedonism, and exceptionalism can there be true transformation in the nation. Due to a lack of faith in action, which is a flaw in our collective will, God's unlimited power at our disposal is not released. Our creeds and deeds are oceans apart. Therefore, life continues on the same destructive trajectory.

Mere talking is not going to change the trajectory. It is going to take real revolutionary action. All across this country, people have substituted talk for action. They have replaced rhetoric for revolution. Politicians are talking; educators are talking; the justice department is talking; churches are talking. Out of all of this talk, very little is getting done to solve the problems of our time. We talk about statistics, data, national debt, and a host of national issues, yet the problems are still unsolved. We analyze, historicize, intellectualize, and often overemphasize the problems but lack the will to solve them. Talk and no action never brings about transformation. Talk and no action never furthers the kingdom of God on earth. It never gets us closer to a more perfect union, nor does it eliminate poverty and homelessness, reform our criminal justice system, or transform the institutions of our society. This is what the apostle Paul meant when he said, "If I speak in the tongues of men or of angels, but do not have love, I am nothing" (1 Cor 13:1). All talk and no action is nothing. James said, "What good is it, my brothers and sisters, if someone claims to have faith but has no deeds? Can such faith save them? Suppose a brother or a sister is without clothes and daily food. If one of you says to them, 'Go in peace; keep warm and well fed,' but does nothing about their physical needs, what good is it? In the same way, faith by itself, if it is not accompanied by action, is dead" (Jas 2:14–17).

Has our faith died upon our lips? "It is one thing to talk about faith, but it is something else entirely to demonstrate it. A man may process to be an expert swimmer, but if he never goes near the water, his claim means very little. James is simply saying that if you say that you have faith, prove it. To use the vernacular of today, 'Put your money where your mouth is.'"[5] While we are having talks, our common enemy continues unabated, killing, stealing, and destroying our nation. While we are having talks, the criminal justice system remains broken, our educational system is failing, prison facilities are busting loose at the seams, our infrastructure is crumbling, and health-care cost and greed are out of control. We are having a lot of talks about these problems, but our actions are far from solving them. Centuries ago, God spoke through the prophet Micah and said, "Do justly, love mercy, and walk humbly with God" (Mic 6:8). Notice God didn't say *talk* justly, *talk* mercy, and *talk* walking humbly with God. No, God said do it. Act on it. Practice it. Take action.

Walk the talk. Demonstrate justice, mercy, and walking humbly with God. Doing the truth is just as important as knowing the truth. James also said, "Let us be doers and not hearers only" (Jas 1:22).

What our nation and the world needs is not more definitions of Christianity but more demonstrations of Christianity. Persuasive talk may sound good; great oration may move our emotions. But if we lack in action, we are no more than what the apostle Paul called "sounding brass and tinkling cymbals" (1 Cor 13:1). We are just keeping up a lot of noise while the evil time in which we live is unredeemed. The power of God must be manifested through our faith in action. Those who are in need are not interested in talking about analysis, percentages, and trends. They are interested in how much we care. Talking and analyzing alone have never met the needs of the masses of people. Our words must motivate us to act; otherwise, they are a farce. Paulo Freire stated, "When a word is deprived of its dimension of action, reflection automatically suffers as well; and the word is changed into idle chatter, into verbalism, into an alienated 'blah.' It becomes an empty word, one which cannot denounce the world, for denunciation is impossible without a commitment to transform, and there is no transformation without action."[6] We must remember that at the day of judgment, Jesus shall say to us, "Well *done*, good and faithful servant" (Matt 25:23; emphasis mine), not well *said.* Therefore, "there is no true word that is not at the same time a praxis."[7] If we say that we have hope and faith in the kingdom of God, this does not "consist in crossing one's arms and waiting. As long as [we] fight, [we are] moved by hope; and if [we] fight with hope, then [we] can wait."[8]

Many people think the problems of the world are so great that the little we do won't make a difference. But if each person does his or her part, this factors out to be a lot in the transformation of the world. Each drop of water makes an ocean. If each person could put words and actions together, our world could be much closer to the manifestation of the kingdom of God. Frederick Douglass stated, "If there is no struggle, there is no progress. Those who profess to favor freedom and yet deprecate agitation are [people] who crops without plowing up the ground; they want rain without thunder and lightning; they want the ocean without the awful roar of its many waters. This struggle may be a moral one, or it may be a physical one, and it may be both moral and physical, but it must be struggle. Power concedes nothing without a demand. It never did and it never will."[9] It is time to move beyond talk to action and create a nation of life, liberty, and the pursuit of happiness. What we need now is for the government, the postmodern church, and the institutions of our society to move beyond rhetoric and act on behalf of justice, peace, and the kingdom of God.

Many centuries ago, God spoke to Moses at Mt. Horeb, saying, "You have stayed long enough at this mountain. Break camp and advance into the hill country of the Amorites; go to all the neighboring peoples in the Arabah, in the mountains, in the western foothills, in the Negev and along the coast, to the land of the Canaanites and to Lebanon, as far as the great river, the Euphrates" (Deut 1:6–8). God was saying to Moses as God is saying to us today, "You have rested at the mountain long enough. You have had enough conferences, workshops, seminars, and banquets. Move from this mountain of confabulation! There are more challenges to meet and more territory to cover. There are more risks to take, battles to fight, and victories to win. You cannot bring about transformation if you don't move beyond confabulation. Furthermore, can't you see your young people are dying? Can't you see your prisons are bursting loose at the seams? Can't you see families are coming apart? Can't you see your schools are war zones? Can't you see immorality has reached new lows? Can't you see your politicians are like wolves, destroying lives for unjust riches, and many preachers are covering up for the politicians, whitewashing everything for them? Can't you see the oppression of the poor and the mistreatment of immigrants? It is time to break camp of *having* church and move on to *becoming* the church. It is time to break camp of *defining* Christianity to *demonstrating* Christianity. It is time to break camp of *membership* to *discipleship*. It is time to break camp of *fear* and move on with *faith in action*. If you want a better future for yourselves, your children, and your children's children, then it is time to break camp and move on!" Somehow, can we hear God speaking to our hearts concerning the crisis in the nation and the world?

To transform America and the world and redeem the evil times in which we live, it is time to move from being an inactive, Bible-toting, hymn-chanting, silent onlooker to a transformer of our times. The kingdom of God is not talk but power, and this power must be put in action to achieve the dream of God on earth. We must recapture the power of the early church, which transformed an empire. Harry Emerson Fosdick said, "If we Christians were worth our salt we could reproduce that now. Did someone come here today saying, 'This is no time for Christian faith!' I tell you this is no time for atheism. This is no time to tell men there is no God, no eternal purpose through life, no goal ahead of it, no sense in it. This is no time for cynicism and skepticism and materialism.... This is a time to see again the deep meanings of the Christian faith."[10]

Our world is in such dire need of the gospel of Jesus Christ that we don't have time for theological and philosophical squabbles. The early church didn't get caught up in petty squabbles because they were too busy operating in the power of the Holy Spirit. A. W. Tozer said,

> The Church began in power, moved in power, and moved just as long as she had power. When she no longer had power she dug in for safety and sought to conserve her gains. But her blessings were like the manna: when they tried to keep it overnight it bred worms and stank. So we have had monasticism, scholasticism, institutionalism; and they have all been indicative of the same thing: absence of spiritual power.... The Church must have power; she must become formidable, a moral force to be reckoned with, if she would regain her lost position of spiritual ascendancy and make her message revolutionizing, conquering thing it once was.[11]

It is going to take spiritual power to transform the American empire. America has been dealing with the ugliness of racism for a long time. Racism keeps raising its ugly head, reminding us that the problem is still systematic. When it seems we are making progress, the nagging hounds of hell come barking again. We react to it, talk about it, diagnosis it, but we consistently fall short in correcting it. The reason is corrective action never gets implemented. America puts a bandage on it to cover it as a quick fix, but the wound is still unhealed, causing pain in the land. Racism must be exposed and eliminated, not covered up in the shroud of religious sanctity. Martin Luther King Jr. stated, "Like a boil that can never be cured as long as it is covered up but must be opened with all its pus-flowing ugliness to the natural medicines of air and light, injustice must likewise be exposed, with all of the tension its exposing creates, to the light of human conscience and the air of national opinion before it can be cured."[12] Going forward as a nation, we must decide what kind of nation we are going to be and not just talk about it but demonstrate it in our government, schools, churches, and institutions of society. America is in an urgent situation. James Russell Lowell said, "Once to every man and nation, comes the moment to decide, in the strife of truth with falsehood, for the good or evil side; some great cause, some great decision, offering each the bloom or blight, and the choice goes by forever, twist that darkness and the light. Then to side with truth is noble, when we share her wretched crust, ere her cause bring fame and profit, and 'tis prosperous to be just; then it is the brave man chooses while the coward stands aside, till the multitude make virtue the faith they had denied."[13]

America either needs to live up to her creed and be true to what is written in the Constitution or admit to being a nation of liars who only talk freedom and justice but never really mean it. The nation cannot afford to postpone making the decision any longer. America must decide now before it is too late. Howard Thurman warns us as a nation, "Unless there is a great rebirth of high and holy moral courage, which will place at the center of our vast power an abiding sense of moral responsibility, both because of our treatment of minorities at home and our arrogance abroad, we may very easily become the most hated nation on earth. No amount of power, wealth, or prestige can stay this judgment. If we would be beloved we must share that kind of spirit as the expression of the true genius of our democratic government."[14]

I do not believe that America is so morally bankrupt that she is incapable of giving herself fully, without reservations, to democracy or to Christianity. I believe it will take the prompting of the church to help America decide about its future. If the church is unwilling to take a stand for justice and democracy, then the nation is truly at risk, especially when America stands at the judgment seat of Christ. Any lukewarm stance, be it church or nation, will be rejected. Before it is too late, America needs to repent and understand that "the profound hunger of our time is not for brotherly words, but brotherly deeds, not for the publishing of brave resolutions, but for the launching of brave experiments. We have seen too much hate in action, cruelty in action, bestiality in action. What America and the world urgently need is love, gentleness, humanity,—in action."[15]

Love in action is surrendering oneself on behalf of others: "Each time a man stands up for an ideal, or acts to improve the lot of others, or strikes out against injustice, he sends forth a tiny ripple of hope, and crossing each other from a million different centers of energy and daring, those ripples build a current that can sweep down the mightiest walls of oppression and resistance."[16] As Americans we have the ability to practice love. When a crisis hits, such as a hurricane, we are willing to forget our differences, our race, class, color, religion, and politics because our survival depends on each other. We are reminded of our common humanity. Therefore, we can no longer just talk about the cancer of racism in our body politic; we must get rid of the cancer before the cancer gets rid of us. We must get rid of it in our policies, in our government, in our schools, on Wall Street and Main Street. We have to treat racism like David treated Goliath. When David went out to fight the giant Goliath, God gave him the victory over the giant. To make sure this giant would never raise his head again against the nation of Israel, David cut off his head. The point I am making is that racism is a nagging giant in our nation, but we refuse to kill it and cut off its head. When I say kill it, I mean we must kill it through our social and national policies to make sure justice, equality, and democracy are the end results. Just talking about it only allows it to return stronger and more determined to turn us over to greater tyranny.

Some states have taken down Confederate monuments and are in the process of deciding what to do with them. Taking down monuments is an action step, but we must encourage states and the nation to go further to get rid of unjust polices that are unfair, unjust, and undemocratic. Monuments are statues of stone, but polices are living documents that regulate people's everyday behavior in society. We must correct the polices. The late William R. Jones, who was my major professor at Florida State University, taught us that "every correction is a change but not every change is a correction." We can change something without correcting it. Taking down monuments is a change, but unless people correct the hatred, bigotry, and bitterness in public polices, which are matters of the heart, these things will manifest themselves in other ways in our nation. Ralph Waldo Emerson said, "What lies behind us and what lies before us are tiny matters compared to what lies within us."[17]

We do have within us the capacity to "cease to do evil, learn to do good, seek justice, rebuke the oppressor; defend the fatherless, and plead for the widow" (Isa 1:16–17). Therefore, we must do more than just talk love, justice, and democracy; we must demonstrate it. Paul reminds us that the kingdom of God is not talk but power, and we need power, spiritual power, to give us the prompting we need to carry out the will of God. It was God's power that freed the children of Israel from the slavery of Egypt, drowning Pharaoh and his army in the Red Sea. It was God's power working through Nehemiah and the people to rebuild the wall around Jerusalem. It was God's power that kept the Jews from being annihilated when Esther went to the king. It was God's power that turned away Job's affliction, giving him double what he had before.

There are numerous examples of God's kingdom being power, not just talk. Paul said, "I am not ashamed of the gospel of Christ, for it is the power of God unto salvation" (Rom 1:16). Paul Tillich states, "Power is the possibility a Being has to actualize itself against the resistance of other beings. If we speak of the power of being-itself we indicate that being affirms itself against nonbeing."[18] Therefore, we have the power to work against all vices of nonbeing. We have power to heal, power to save, power to set free, power to transform, power to turn darkness into light, power to turn tears into testimonies, power to turn a crisis into a celebration, and power to rise up and make this old world a new world.

The kingdom of God is not talk but power! Walter Rauschenbusch says, "Here we come back to our previous proposition that the Kingdom of God is the commonwealth of co-operative service and that the most common form of sinful selfishness is the effort to escape from labor."[19] Unless we put labor where faith is, there is no need to talk, because the kingdom of God is power. Fosdick sums it up this way:

> To be a Christian means to take in your strong hands the love-ethic and go out into this pagan world to live by it, believe in it, adventure on it, sacrifice for it, until we make it victorious in the institutions of mankind. And that is costly. Yet difficult and costly as it is, power in the hands of love is always the most beautiful thing in the world. And any kind of power—personal charm, intelligence, skill, leadership, possessions—in the hands of love is the most convincing thing in the world.[20]

If the church doesn't learn anything else from the early Christian movement, it is my hope and prayer that the church never forgets that the kingdom of God is not talk but power!

ENDNOTES

[1] Herbert V. Prochnow, *The Speaker's Book of Illustrations* (Grand Rapids: Baker Book House, 1974), 126.

[2] A. W. Tozer, *Man: The Dwelling Place of God* (San Francisco: Fig Publisher, 2012), 137.

[3] Ibid., 119.

[4] Walter Rauschenbusch, (Christianizing the Social Order (1912)), *Walter Rauschenbusch: Selected Writings*, Sources of American Spirituality, ed. Winthrop S. Hudson (Mahwah NJ: Paulist Press, 1984), 188–89.

[5] George Sweeting, *Faith That Works: A Study of the Book of James* (Chicago: Moody Press, 1973, 1983), 66.

[6] Paulo Freire, *Pedagogy of the Oppressed* (New York: The Continuum Publishing Company, 1993), 68.

[7] Ibid., 68.

[8] Ibid., 73.

[9] Frederick Douglass, *The Frederick Douglass Papers, Series Three: Speeches, Debates, and Interviews*, vol.3: 1855-63, ed. John W. Blassingame and John R. McKivigan (New Haven: Yale University Press, 1985), 204.

[10] Harry Emerson Fosdick, *Answers to Real Problems: Harry Emerson Fosdick Speaks to Our Time*, ed. Mark E. Yurs (Eugene OR: Wipf & Stock Publishers, 2008), 16.

[11] A. W. Tozer, *Paths to Power: Living in the Spirit's Fullness* (Chicago: Moody Bible Institute, 1940), 7–8.

[12] Martin Luther King Jr., "Letter from Birmingham City Jail" (April 16, 1963), cited in *A Testament of Hope, The Essential Writings of Martin Luther King, Jr.*, ed. James Melvin Washington (San Francisco: Harper & Row, 1986), 295.

[13] James Russell Lowell, *Baptist Hymnal*, 2008, #538.

[14] Howard Thurman, *Deep River and the Negro Spiritual Speaks of Life and Death* (Richmond IN: Friends United Press, 1975), 59.

[15] Fred D. Wentzel, *Epistle to White Christians* (Philadelphia: The Christian Education Press, 1948), 91.

[16] Robert F. Kennedy, N.U.S.A.S. "Day of Affirmation" speech, University of Cape Town, South Africa, June 6, 1966.

[17] Henry Stanley Haskins, *Meditations in Wall Street* (New York: William Morrow & Company, 1940), 131.

[18] Paul Tillich, *The Courage to Be* (New Haven: Yale University Press, 1952), 179.

[19] Rauschenbusch, [title from note 4 should go here], 202.

[20] Fosdick, *Answers to Real Problems*, 49.

CHAPTER FOUR

FAITH IN ACTION

Faith is to believe what you do not see;
the reward of this faith is to see what you believe.

—Saint Augustine

I heard a story many years ago about a man who was walking on
a narrow path. Not paying attention, he slipped and fell off a cliff but
was able to catch hold of a branch that broke his fall. Realizing he
couldn't hang on to the branch forever, he called for help. God spoke
to the man: "Have faith! Let go of the branch." The man refused to
let go and called out to see if there was someone else up there to help
him. The moral of the story is the man refused to let go. He refused
to put faith in action. Think of the many people who pray to God
for help and healing but refuse to let go of the situation. They pray
to God to help their children, their community, and their nation but
refuse to let go. For God to save us, we must let go—of our situations,
our circumstances, our hatred, pride, addiction, prejudices, racism,
and everything that divides the human family—and put our faith
in action. God cannot perform for us what we desire when we are
unwilling to let go. Without letting go we cannot see and experience
the miracle.

To clarify, when I say "let go," I don't mean acquiesce. We must
do our part and trust God and leave the results in his hand. Whatever
progress human beings have made to make the world more just
and humane did not happen by being silent onlookers. People got
involved. With human action and God's power working together, they
have made their faith count. To progress toward a world less unjust,

less inhumane, and less unloving, we must move beyond passivity to participation. Oftentimes we don't know the strength within us until situations and circumstances pressure us to act, and when we act, we find out that the solution to our problem was already within us, waiting for us to put faith in action. It is a truism that we are like teabags, thinking we are not worth much until we have been through some hot water.

God often allows us to be put in hot water situations to draw out of us what is in us. But when we refuse to put our faith in action, we cannot experience the power of God in our situation, just like a boat that is never put in water cannot experience sailing. We were made to experience God. Just like a motor moves a boat across the water, faith moves God to act on our behalf. Faith, then, is not an abstract concept that excludes action, and action doesn't exclude doubt. Faith takes in doubt and still makes the risk. Faith is risk-taking. Paul Tillich said, "Living faith includes the doubt about itself, the courage to take this doubt into itself, and the risk of courage."[1] Only when we risk can we know the manifestation of God operating in and through us. Tillich further stated, "Without the manifestation of God in [humans] the question of God and faith in God are not possible. There is no faith without our participation."[2] To have transformation in the human situation, there must be participation of the engagement of faith. Engagement of faith is to have the courage to act even when doubtful about acting.

Simon Peter, one of Jesus's most outspoken and impulsive disciples, put his faith in action when he wasn't sure of the outcome. Peter was not perfect by a long shot, but he did release his faith, and he got results. When Peter saw Jesus walking on water, he said, "Lord, if it is You, command me to come to You on the water" (Matt 14:28). Peter stepped out on faith and actually walked on water. He didn't worry about how it was done; he did it by moving out on faith, and he experienced a miracle. On another occasion Peter had fished all day and didn't catch anything. He was instructed by Jesus to cast out his nets again: "Simon answered, 'Master, we've worked hard all night and haven't caught anything. But because you say so, I will let down the nets'" (Luke 5:5). Peter was doubtful about letting the nets down again. He was an experienced fisherman, and his experience told him that the fish were not biting this night. But Peter decided to let the nets down again, either to prove he was right or to prove that Jesus was right. Nevertheless, he took the risk, though doubtful that the fish were there.

Notice what Peter said: "Because you say, I will let down the nets." Peter acted on his faith in Jesus. Though he was doubtful about the outcome, he still had the courage to obey. When we act, doubt gets swallowed up in our obedience, and faith gets us results. Many times we may not understand why the Lord is leading us to do certain things, but we should still obey the word of the Lord. Because of Peter's faith and courage, he caught so many fish that his net broke. He called for help to the others in another ship, and the ships began to sink. The miracle of our blessing is tied up in the release of our faith. Once we have the courage to release faith into action, the results are staggering. Tillich said, "Faith accepts 'in spite of'; and out of the 'in spite of' of faith the 'in spite of' of courage is born. Faith is not a theoretical affirmation of something uncertain, it is the existential acceptance of something transcending ordinary experience. Faith is not an opinion but a state. It is the state of being grasped by the power of being which transcends everything that is and in which everything that is participates."[3]

Therefore, in spite of our limitations and overwhelming circumstances, putting faith in action bridges the possible with the impossible. Earlier, I mentioned Nick Vujicic, who was born without arms and legs. Vujicic could have lived life in self-pity, anger, and bitterness like many people are doing today. Instead, he decided to live a life of faith, and God has used him to speak to millions around the world. He has his own business. He is the author of an international best-selling book *Unstoppable: The Incredible Power of Faith in Action*. He is married and now has children. Vujicic's life is a testament of what God can do despite our limitations and circumstances. He said, "To begin to understand this, simply keep in mind that this man with no arms and no legs travels the world, reaching out to millions of people, while blessed with joy and love beyond measure. I am as imperfect as anyone you will ever meet. I have good days and bad. Challenges rise up and knock me flat on occasion. Yet I know that where I am weak, God is strong, and when we put faith into action, we are unstoppable."[4]

Now, if Vujicic can rise up and make an impact on the world with his physical limitations, what is our excuse? Listen to his wisdom:

> Will I always get what I want? No! But I will always get what God wants. The same is true for you. Whether you are a Christian or not, you must never think that believing in something is enough. You can believe in your dreams, but you have to take action to make them happen.... You may have had challenges in your career, your relationships, or your health. Maybe you have been mistreated, abused, or discriminated against. All those things that have happened to you do define you or your life if you fail to take action to define yourself. You can believe in your talents. You can believe that you have love to give. You can believe that you can overcome your illness or disability. But that belief on its own won't bring positive change in your life. You must put it into action.... It's said that the universe rewards action, and that certainly has been true for me.[5]

Putting faith in action certainly has it rewards. It is not only true for Vujicic but for social movements as well. The action of three movements in the West that put faith in action have been rewarding not only for England but America as well. England and America were put on a trajectory to help move the moral and racial justice needle further. The evangelical movement of England and the abolitionist movement and the civil rights movement of America were the leaven in the social transformation loaf of the two nations. Each movement inspired the next movement by putting faith in action. These three movements are highlighted because they have lasted longer than subsequent movements that started and then phased out. The three highlighted movements have impacted the lives of millions of people, and the moral and spiritual state of Europe and America are better because of it. Think of where we would be if these three movements had not taken place. These movements started off small with a few participants, but over time they became a moral and spiritual force of which their demands could not be denied. Their faith in action brought about fundamental moral and social change.

However, the demonic forces that were arrested by these three movements have escaped from their containment to deliver us over to a greater tyranny. Unless we come together and arrest these forces again, we may not get another opportunity to do so. Personalities of the past put their faith in action and transformed the world. People like John Wesley and William Wilberforce of the evangelical movement of England; William Lloyd Garrison, Frederick Douglass, and Harriet Beecher Stowe of the abolitionist movement; Rosa Parks, Martin Luther King Jr., John and Bobby Kennedy, and countless others of the civil rights movement—all operated in faith, and we need personalities today to do likewise. These demonic forces must not only be arrested again but given the death penalty and an immediate execution date. The forces of racism, injustice, exploitation, marginalization, and all the xenophobic forces that divide and separate us need to be given an execution date so their influence will never again plague our nation and the world. But it is going to take faith in action to achieve this. It was done in the past and can be done again if we truly love democracy and freedom.

In the past the moral conditions in England were so bad that faith in action could not be a private affair. Diane Severance wrote, "Morally, the country was becoming increasingly decadent. Drunkenness was rampant; gambling was so extensive that one historian described England as 'One vast casino.' Newborns were exposed in the streets; 97% of the infant poor in the workhouses died as children.

Bear baiting and cock fighting were accepted sports, and tickets were sold to public executions as to a theater. The slave trade brought material gain to many while further degrading their souls. Bishop Berkeley wrote that morality and religion in Britain had collapsed 'to a degree that was never known in any Christian country.'"[6]

John Wesley helped to liberate England from its cesspool of iniquity. Due to his public faith in action, Wesley went through unimaginable suffering, including excessive taunts, threats, and physical violence. Nevertheless, his faith was stronger than the fleeting voices of disapproval. Just like George Whitefield inspired John Wesley, it was John Wesley who inspired William Wilberforce to take a stance against the slave trade. The faith in action of George Whitefield, John Wesley, and William Wilberforce spread across England, and millions responded to the social reform. "The revival cut across denominational lines and touched every class of society. England itself was transformed by the revival. In 1928 Archbishop Davidson wrote that 'Wesley practically changed the outlook and even the character of the English nation.'"[7] Faith in action transformed the whole nation of England, and through Wilberforce's influence in the government, slavery was also abolished in England. "Wilberforce's sons believed their father's calling was to bring to the upper classes the message that Wesley had brought to the lower—to 'raise his voice in the high places of the land; and do within the church, and near the throne, what Wesley had accomplished in the meeting, and amongst the multitude.'"[8]

It is of great importance to reach the upper class as well as the lower class. The upper class and the rich are the ones who hold the power and resources, and transformation cannot be complete without the power brokers in any nation. In this sense, putting faith in action is a doubled-edged sword. Hannah More wrote, "Reformation must begin with the Great, or it will never be effectual. Their example is the fountain whence the vulgar draw their habits, actions, and character. To expect to reform the poor while the opulent are corrupt, is to throw odours into the stream while the springs are poisoned. If, therefore, the Rich and Great will not, from a liberal spirit of doing right, and from a Christian spirit of fearing God, abstain from those offenses, for which the poor are to suffer fines and imprisonments, effectual good cannot be done."[9] This is the reason we must reach the powerful and the powerless in our efforts to transform the nation. We cannot neglect the political process because we need just laws to help in the transformation of the nation; political involvement is necessary.

The evangelical movement of England inspired the abolitionist movement of America. Since slavery was outlawed in England, its influence reached America. Slavery was the institutional misery of millions of blacks, and it was the immoral, undemocratic snare of America. Personalities like William Lloyd Garrison started a newspaper called *Liberator*, through which he called for the immediate manumission of slaves and their complete equality. His faith in action was getting the message out about human bondage. Garrison hated slavery, and he did his best to arouse the slumbering land of complacency and acceptance of human bondage: "I hate slavery as I hate nothing else in this world. It is not only a crime, but the sum of all criminality; not only a sin, but the sin of sins against Almighty God. I cannot be at peace with it at any time, to any extent, under any circumstances."[10] Like John Wesley of England, who suffered persecution and threats for his faith in action, Garrison suffered the same. At times he thought his cause was futile with only a few antislavery participants willing to make the sacrifice to bring to an end this gross practice of slavery. Garrison stated, "Are we enough to make a revolution? No, but we are enough to begin one, and, once begun, it never can be turned back. I am for the revolution, we're I utterly alone. I am there because I must be there. I must cleave to the right. I cannot choose but obey the voice of God."[11] Garrison was willing to put his faith in action, and because of his efforts, many more people began to listen. Looking back on his life against human bondage, Garrison stated, "In seizing the 'trump of God,' I had indeed to blow 'a jarring blast'—but it was necessary to wake up a nation then slumbering in a lap of moral death. Thanks be to God, that blast was effectual; it pierced the ears of the deaf, it started the lethargic from their criminal sleep, and it shook the land as a leaf is shaken by the wind."[12]

We never know who we may inspire when we put our faith in action. Garrison's trumpet blast was heard by Frederick Douglass, who had just escaped from slavery. Like Garrison, Douglass fought hard against slavery. He gave his life to see slavery's demise. Douglass put his faith in action and became an eloquent orator against slavery. Douglass started his own newspaper, contributing to ending this immoral practice. Having been a slave himself, Douglass could speak and write with authority about the horrors of slavery. Douglass challenged America to free itself from this godless practice before the weight of heaven came crushing down on the young nation. In a Fourth of July speech, Douglass spoke these words:

> My subject, then, fellow-citizens, is American slavery. I shall see this day and its popular characteristics from the slave's point of view. Standing there identified with the American bondman, making his wrongs mine, I do not hesitate to declare, with all my soul, that the character and conduct of this nation never looked blacker to me than on this 4th of July! Whether we turn to the declarations of the past, or to the professions of the present, the conduct of the nation seems equally hideous and revolting. America is false to the past, false to the present, and solemnly binds herself to be false to the future. Standing with God and the crushed and bleeding slave on this occasion, I will, in the name of humanity which is outraged, in the name of liberty which is fettered, in the name of the constitution and the Bible which are disregarded and trampled upon, dare to call in question and to denounce, with all the emphasis I can command, everything that serves to perpetuate slavery-the great sin and shame of America!
>
> What, to the American slave, is your 4th of July? I answer; a day that reveals to him, more than all other days in the year, the gross injustice and cruelty to which he is the constant

victim. To him, your celebration is a sham; your boasted liberty, an unholy license; your national greatness, swelling vanity; your sounds of rejoicing are empty and heartless; your denunciation of tyrants, brass fronted impudence; your shouts of liberty and equality, hollow mockery; your prayers and hymns, your sermons and thanksgivings, with all your religious parade and solemnity, are, to Him, mere bombast, fraud, deception, impiety, and hypocrisy-a thin veil to cover up crimes which would disgrace a nation of savages. There is not a nation on the earth guilty of practices more shocking and bloody than are the people of the United States, at this very hour. Go where you may, search where you will, roam through all the monarchies and despotisms of the Old World, travel through South America, search out every abuse, and when you have found the last, lay your facts by the side of the everyday practices of this nation, and you will say with me, that, for revolting barbarity and shameless hypocrisy, America reigns without a rival.[13]

Not only did Douglass put his faith in action against slavery; he influenced Abraham Lincoln to throw his weight behind the effort to eliminate slavery from the land. Abraham Lincoln had to come to the conclusion that our land could not remain half-slave and half-free. Lincoln stated, "A house divided against itself cannot stand. I believe this government cannot endure permanently half-slave and half-free. I do not expect the Union to be dissolved—I do not expect the house to fall—but I do expect it will cease to be divided. It will become all one thing or all the other."[14] To stop the spread of slavery, the conflict between the North and South had to be settled. Sadly, the conflict ended in war, and Lincoln signed the Emancipation Proclamation, ending American slavery. Through the efforts of Garrison, Douglass, Lincoln, and countless others putting their faith in action, America became a true land of democracy, though it was anemic for black Americans.

America had come a long way in democracy as a nation while black Americans were freed but still not free. Black Americans had no civil rights and were discriminated against in every way. The North and the South were still divided over black people. Injustice, humiliation, marginalization, and exploitation were common practice against blacks. Mob violence against blacks was common in the South, and very rarely, if at all, did any white person pay for their crimes against black people. Efforts were made in the struggle for civil rights, but it wasn't until a woman named Rosa Parks decided to put her faith in action that the civil rights movement took off like wildfire. This led to the leadership of Martin Luther King Jr., who challenged America to come full circle in democracy. Leading over 250,000 people to Washington, D.C., to advocate for full citizenship rights, King stated, "We have also come to this hallowed spot to remind America of the fierce urgency of Now. This is no time to engage in the luxury of cooling off or to take the tranquilizing drug of gradualism. Now is the time to make real the promises of democracy."[15] Through much struggle and sacrifice America again made great strides toward democracy and decency. King and countless others put their faith in action, and America is better off because of it.

When we decide to put our faith in action and struggle against wrong, evil, and injustice, not only are we in the process of bettering our nation, but we are also bettering our world, which really needs a nation to show the just way, the righteous way, and the democratic way. We should never take for granted putting faith in action. We never know who is watching and who we are influencing. It is difficult for people to listen to Christians when they don't put their faith in action. Nick Vujicic stated,

> God wants us to do the right thing, and that includes never letting another person suffer if you can help it. The traveler found by the Good Samaritan had been bullied, beaten, and robbed. Jesus didn't waffle on what He expects us to do if we find someone in that situation. As God's children, we

are expected to help one another. Standing by and watching someone be harassed, pushed around, ridiculed, and marginalized is not Christian behavior, neither is it humane.... The Good Samaritan didn't just offer a word of encouragement. He interrupted his own journey, treated the wounds of the beaten man, took him to a safe place, and made sure he was taken care of until he recovered. The Bible offers no description of the robbery victim, and I think that's because Jesus wants us to be good Samaritans to anyone in need, whether they like us or not.[16]

Finally, our nation, the church, the community, and the world are in desperate need of people who say they love to put their faith in action. The apostle James said, "What good is it, my brothers and sisters, if someone claims to have faith but has no deeds? Can such faith save them? Suppose a brother or a sister is without clothes and daily food. If one of you says to them, 'Go in peace; keep warm and well fed,' but does nothing about their physical needs, what good is it? In the same way, faith by itself, if it is not accompanied by action, is dead" (Jas 2:14–17).

ENDNOTES

[1] Paul Tillich, *Dynamics of Faith* (New York: Harper & Row, 1957), 102.

[2] Ibid., 100.

[3] Paul Tillich, *The Courage to Be* (New Haven: Yale University Press, 1952), 172–173.

[4] Nick Vujicic, *Unstoppable: The Incredible Power of Faith in Action* (New York: WaterBrook Press, 2012), 3.

[5] Ibid., 8–9, 15.

[6] Diane Severance, "Evangelical Revival in England," *Christianity.com*, timeline 1701–1800, first published April 28, 2010. http://www.christianity.com/church/church-history/timeline/1701-1800/evangelical-revival-in-england-11630228.html

[7] Ibid.

[8] Herbert Sclossberg, cited from *VictorianWeb.org*, Evangelical Movement in the Church of England, part five of "Religious Revival and the Transformation of English Sensibilities in the Early 19th Century." http://www.victorianweb.org/religion/herb5.html

[9] Hannah More, "Thoughts on the Importance of the Manners of the Great to General Society, and an Estimate of the Religion of the Fashionable World" (London: T. Cadell and W. Davies, Strand, 1809), 78.

[10] William Lloyd Garrison, *The Words of Garrison: A Centennial Selection (1805–1905) of Characteristic Sentiments from the Writing of William Lloyd Garrison* (New York: Riverside Press, 1905), 11.

[11] Ibid., 5.

[12] Ibid., 6.

[13] Frederick Douglass, "The Meaning of the 4th for the Negro," speech, Rochester, New York, July 5, 1852.

[14] Abraham Lincoln, "House Divided" speech, Springfield, Illinois, June 16, 1858.

[15] Martin Luther King Jr., "I Have a Dream," speech, Washington, D.C., August 28, 1963.

[16] Nick Vujicic, *Unstoppable: The Incredible Power of Faith in Action* (New York: WaterBrook Press, 2012), 163–64.

CHAPTER FIVE

BOLD FAITH

Have I not commanded you? Be strong and of good courage;
do not be afraid, nor be dismayed, for the LORD your God is with
you wherever you.

—Joshua 1:9

No task can be accomplished without boldness. No war can be won without boldness. No mountain can be climbed without boldness. No giant can be conquered without boldness. No demon can be overcome without boldness. No transformation can happen without boldness. To do God's will on earth as it is in heaven requires boldness. The greatest hinderance to advancing God's kingdom is cowardice. Too many people, especially Christians, have the spirit of fear, and this fear keeps them from boldly standing up and correcting the wrongs of society. Robert Kennedy said, "Few [people] are willing to brave the disapproval of their fellows, the censure of their colleagues, the wrath of their society. Moral courage is a rarer commodity than bravery in battle or great intelligence. Yet it is the one essential, vital quality of those who seek to change a world which yields most painfully to change."[1]

To arrest the unjust economic, social, and political structures of life requires boldness of faith. How can we claim to be Christians and followers of the Prince of Peace when we are fearful of correcting the wrongs of society? How can we claim to be the church of God and allow evil to run rampant in our communities and nation? Without a bold faith, the risk we need to take to conquer the world for Christ won't be conquered. Think of what we could accomplish for the kingdom of God if we were not paralyzed by fear. Therefore, before humanity is plunged into nuclear annihilation, we need to conquer our fear and develop a bold faith to move from *chronos*, the present situation, to *kairos*, the right time to act before it is too late.

To get rid of our morbid fear, we must trace the root of it and start there to free ourselves from it. Traditional theology traces fear to the broken relationship between God and humanity. When Adam and Eve disobeyed God and hid themselves, fear had overcome them. Fear, then, is rooted in our disobedience and the consequence of it, which is death. Since this break in relationship between God and humanity, fear has become an ontological phenomenon. Humanity fears death and the unknown. And whatever we fear, we tend to run from it, and sometimes we are paralyzed by it. Paul Tillich calls this pathological anxiety that produces fear:

> Fear and anxiety are distinguished but not separated. They are immanent within each other: The sting of fear is anxiety, and anxiety strives toward fear. Fear is being afraid of something, a pain, the rejection by a person or a group, the loss of something or somebody, the moment of dying. But in the anticipation of the threat originating in these things, it is not the negativity itself which they will bring upon the subject that is frightening but the anxiety about the possible implications of this negativity. The outstanding example—and more than an example—is the fear of dying…. The dreams in Hamlet's soliloquy, "to be or not to be," which we may have after death and which make cowards of us all are frightful not because of their manifest content but because of their power to symbolize the threat of nothingness, in religious terms of "eternal death."[2]

Due to the fact that we are fearful of nonbeing and the anxiety of these powerful symbols of death, we recoil back into our perceived safety to avoid facing frightening situations of life. "The human mind is not only, as Calvin has said, a permanent factory of idols, it is also a permanent factory of fears—the first in order to escape God, the second in order to escape anxiety; and there is a relation between the two."[3] Fear and its powerful symbols are keeping us from acting with faith against oppression, injustice, and inhumanity. The enemy of our soul, Satan, uses these powerful symbols of nonbeing to create the anxiety that moves toward fear to maintain his hold on world systems. Until we conquer the symbols of death within us, the world shall continue in a downward spiral toward destruction. Nations shall continue to rise up against nations, and war and bloodshed shall continue to be our constant companions. Dehumanization and its effect upon the human spirit can only be conquered by bold faith in God.

Herein lies the hope of humanity: bold faith united with the spirit of God. God and humanity work together to straighten out crooked places and smooth down rough edges so justice and equality can roll down like waters and righteousness like a mighty stream. The cooperation between God and humanity is necessary if we are to see structural changes in society. Too often we put transformation and liberation of situations on God's shoulders while we stand idly by as sideline spectators. Bold faith is not standing on the sideline; it is not non-participation or a hands-off approach to life. Bold faith is active involvement in present situations for future transformation. God wants humanity to do its part. Bad theology has taught putting situations and circumstances in God's hand while folding our hand. Much of the world is in a colossal mess because we have shifted our responsibility solely to God while we sit back and sing hymns, worship, and pray, expecting God to clean up the mess without having a broom and mop in our hands to assist.

When Moses and the children of Israel were at the Red Sea and Pharaoh and his army were pursuing from behind, Moses was in a crisis. The Red Sea was before them; Pharaoh was behind them; hills and mountains were on each side of them. What were they to do? Moses and the children of Israel thought crying out to the Lord would rectify the situation, but God said something profound that we need to hear today: "Why are you crying out to me? Tell the Israelites to move on. Raise your staff and stretch out your hand over the sea to divide the water so that the Israelites can go through the sea on dry ground" (Exod 14:15–16). God wanted Moses to demonstrate bold faith and do the possible; God would do the impossible. God through Christ is saying the same to the postmodern church: "Why are you crying to me? Raise up your faith, stretch out what you have in your hand, and you shall see the transformation of the situation. Use what you have to correct oppression, uproot racism and sexism, feed the hungry, clothe the naked, provide shelter for the homeless, heal the broken-hearted, release the captives, recover the sight of the blind, and set at liberty them that are bruised. These things are possible when we practice consistent bold faith.

However, when we won't do our part, the world and its systems remain the same. Bold faith is necessary in our individual and collective lives. Don't expect any transformation, deliverance, and achievement without the practice of bold faith. Bold faith may go against the prevailing opinion of society. It may be out of step with the status quo. It may be out of line with the political platform, and it may transgress traditional and newly formed boundaries. But bold faith is necessary to win the world for Christ. Scripture teaches, "Without faith it is impossible to please God" (Heb 11:6). A person who prays to pass a test but won't study probably won't pass. A farmer who prays for a harvest but planted no seeds won't see a harvest. A congregation that prays for numerical growth but refuses to evangelize won't see growth. Oppressed people who won't struggle against their oppression won't experience liberation. The point here is don't expect God to do for us what we refuse to do for ourselves. Bold faith is not waiting until God's hand is visible but acting when God's hand is invisible; not acting when the sun is shining but acting when darkness has enveloped us; not waiting for the supernatural to break in on the natural and force nations and civilizations to chart a different course but demonstrating bold faith and leaving the end results in God's hand.

God through Christ is calling for us to practice bold faith because "God did not give us the spirit of fear but of power, love, and a sound mind" (2 Tim 1:7). Therefore, the spirit of fear does not come from God, and since it does not come from God, we can overcome fear. The spirit of God gives us the courage to act within threatening situations of nonbeing. Paul Tillich stated, "Courage is strength of mind, capable of conquering whatever threatens the attainment of the highest good. It is united with wisdom, the virtue which represents the unity of the four cardinals virtues (the two others being temperance and justice)."[4] As long as we have a relationship with God through Jesus Christ, we have the power to overcome our object of fear. Peter and John overcame their fear and faced the religious leaders of their day and had the courage to speak truth to power. Notice what the scripture says about Peter and John: "Now when they saw the boldness of Peter and John, and perceived that they were uneducated and untrained men, they marveled. And they realized that they had been with Jesus" (Acts 4:13). Relationship with God through Christ is key to having boldness. Peter and John were not theologically trained; they were not philosophically educated; they were ordinary men who had been with Jesus, which gave them the boldness to be a witness in spite of the consequences of doing so in Jesus's name. The world marvels at our boldness when we stand against the prevailing opinion of society. When we are bold and speak truth to power despite the threat of nonbeing, others take notice. God through Christ gives us the boldness to face our fears and conquer them through love. Love and courage are inextricably tied together in demonstrating bold faith.

When a child is trapped under an overturned, burning car, there are cases in which parents faced the fear with courage and saved the child. Later, the parent was asked, "How did you have the courage and strength to pick up the car and save the child?" It is simple: "There is no fear in love; but perfect love casts out fear, because fear involves torment. But he who fears has not been made perfect in love" (1 John 4:18). The parent's love for the child moved the parent to act with courage to overcome the fear of nonbeing. This is not to say that courage doesn't take under consideration the dangers and miscalculation of our actions, but we won't ever know unless we have the courage to act. "Courage listens to reason and carries out the intentions of the mind. It is the strength of the soul to win victory in ultimate danger, like the martyrs of the Old Testament who are enumerated in Hebrews 11. Courage gives consolation, patience, and experience and becomes indistinguishable from faith and hope."[5]

Although we have faith in God, it takes courage of the mind to do what is necessary to transform situations and circumstances. For instance, when David set out to face the giant Goliath, he had faith in God, but he needed courage to face this threatening giant. When King Saul and the other soldiers were too paralyzed by fear to stand against Goliath, David demonstrated bold faith in the midst of threatening nonbeing. Goliath was the object of Israel's fear, but because of David's love of God and his people, David had to first overcome the object of fear in his mind before acting upon it. With courage the object that creates the fear now can be overcome. Tillich says, "Courage can meet every object of fear, because it is an object and makes participation possible. Courage can take the fear produced by a definite object into itself, because this object, however frightful it may be, has a side with which it participates in us and we in it. One can say that as long as there is an object of fear love in the sense of participation can conquer fear."[6] Unless we are willing to act in the midst of our object of fear, our love has not been made perfect. Perfect love creates the boldness we need to act despite facing nonbeing. Nick Vujicic stated, "Faith in Action comes down to love. I love you so much that I care enough about you to serve you and help you and lend an ear, to inspire you and encourage you. It always comes back to love. We have the power to love without limits, and we need to activate that love, not just to fulfill our purpose, but to play a part in seeing the whole world come to a peace and fulfillment in life."[7]

We gain great inspiration in biblical history from Daniel and his three companions who were carried away into Babylonian exile. They demonstrated bold faith in the midst of their situation. The story is found in the third chapter of the book of Daniel. Shadrach, Meshach, and Abednego were caught in a world of oppression, evil, and injustice. Violence and death were the consequences of noncompliance to the law of the land. The nation of Israel was defeated by the Babylonians. While in exile Shadrach, Meshach, and Abednego could have easily allowed fear to cause them to denounce God to survive in a culture of idolatry. They could have easily forgotten God because of their position and status in the Babylonian Empire. They could have easily embraced the gods of colonialism, materialism, and arrogant individualism like people are doing in this postmodern time. But these three young men did not allow what was happening to them and around them to lose faith in God. In fact, it drew them closer to God. They had bold faith in an idolatrous, stubborn world, and when the stubborn world tested their bold faith, they acted with courage. They didn't change their character, their commitment, nor their godly faith to fit within the Babylonian culture. They practiced a bold faith of radical monotheism against cultural polytheism.

When King Nebuchadnezzar passed a new policy that all people and their religions would come under one umbrella and must worship the king's god, the three companions of Daniel demonstrated remarkable boldness of faith. At the sound of the music, all the people were to bow down and worship the king's god. Those who refuse to comply would be torn into the furnace. Bow or burn. They would be facing the unimaginable horror of nonbeing. All of the people were willing to bow because "the threat of nonbeing to man's ontic self-affirmation is absolute in the threat of death, relative in the threat of fate. But the relative threat is a threat only because in its background stands the absolute threat. Fate would not produce inescapable anxiety without death behind it."[8] When the music was played, everybody bowed because they did not want their patriotism called into question, nor did they want to be thrown into the fiery furnace.

But Shadrach, Meshach, and Abednego did not worry about public opinion or about being accused of being unpatriotic. They demonstrated bold faith in a higher patriotism that even the threat of death could not shake. The king had the furnace turned up seven times hotter than normal. The threat of nonbeing was made manifest to show the inescapable possibility of any salvation. Whenever the enemy of faith cannot get us to bow to whatever is wrong, evil, and unjust, the attacks will increase to get us to give in to demands. It is sad today that the faith of too many Christians is so weak that it can be blown in whatever direction the enemy blows it. Their faith has no backbone. But the faith of Shadrach, Meshach, and Abednego said no to majority opinion, to going along to get along, and to a national policy that was out of harmony with the law of God. Listen to the bold faith of these young men who spoke truth to power: "O Nebuchadnezzar, we have no need to answer you in this matter. If that *is the case*, our God whom we serve is able to deliver us from the burning fiery furnace, and He will deliver *us* from your hand, O king. But if not, let it be known to you, O king, that we do not serve your gods, nor will we worship the gold image which you have set up" (Dan 3:16–18).

These young men believed God could deliver them from the burning furnace, but if God decided not to deliver them, they still had absolute faith in God. In order words, they trusted God above the consequences of death. Paul Tillich calls this, "The courage to take meaninglessness into itself presupposes a relation to the ground of being which we have called 'absolute faith.'" When we have absolute faith, we put total trust in God with the assurance that God will eventually save us eternally. Therefore, "Absolute faith and its consequence, the courage that takes the radical doubt, the doubt about God, unto itself, transcend the theistic idea of God,"[9] and still declare an unshakable bold faith in God. Absolute faith in God takes under consideration the uncertainty of any outcomes, yet it is willing to declare as a suffering Job, "I know my redeemer lives" (Job 19:25). The three young men put their faith in God and left the outcome in God's hand. Because they practiced bold faith, they were thrown into the fiery furnace. God, who is always watching his own, had an angel waiting on these young men to deliver them out of the furnace.

Absolute faith rests on the fact that God doesn't prevent our troubles but meets us in our troubles to deliver us. And if God allows us to perish on this side of time because of our faith, this same faith gives us the assurance that we have salvation in eternity based upon the Word of God. These young men were delivered, and this deliverance not only transformed the king to believe in the God of Shadrach, Meshach, and Abednego; it brought others to faith as well.

The same happened in the case of Daniel. When King Darius made a law that no one should pray to any other man or God for thirty days, Daniel decided not to obey the law, boldly praying to God as he always had done. Although the law was an elaborate trick by those who were envious and jealous of Daniel, Daniel demonstrated bold faith in God, and due to Daniel's boldness, God brought King Darius to salvation. Sometimes it is necessary to practice civil disobedience to show a greater obedience to God. We never know how many will be led to the faith by our bold actions. We never know how many people could be transformed by our bold faith. If we are going to redeem the times in which we live, we must have bold faith, like Daniel, Shadrach, Meshach, and Abednego. We must have bold faith, like the apostles, who declared, "We ought to obey God rather than men" (Acts 5:29). Think what could happen in our times if we would practice bold faith. Bold faith conquers kingdoms, receives promises, stops lions' mouths, quenches raging fires, makes enemies into footstools, turns sickness into health, raises the dead to new life, and transforms nations and civilizations.

In American history there are outstanding personalities who showed bold faith in the midst of imminent danger. My list is by no means exhaustive. America would not be the nation she is today without the demonstration of those who showed great boldness. Listen to the words of Patrick Henry:

> We are not weak if we make a proper use of those means which the God of nature hath placed in our power. Three millions of people armed in the holy cause of liberty, and in such a

country as that which we possess, are invincible by any force which our enemy can send against us. Besides, sir, we shall not fight our battles alone. There is a just God who presides over the destinies of nations and who will raise up friends to fight our battles for us. The battle, sir, is not to the strong alone; it is to the vigilant, the active, the brave.... I know not what course others may take, but as for me, give me liberty or give me death![10]

Consider, also, Harriet Tubman, who was born into American slavery. Though she escaped, she went back many times to free others from bondage. She was affectionately called "Moses" because she led dozens of slaves to freedom with the assistance of the Underground Railroad. Tubman risked her life over and over again to gain for others what she had gained for herself—freedom! She braved every danger and overcame every obstacle. With a price on her head, amid danger, hound dogs, slave catchers, traders, swamps, and the nocturnal perils of the journey, Tubman demonstrated such bold faith that she is now an American icon. What makes her iconic is her stunning courage and selflessness. She risked her life on behalf of others. Her work during and after the Civil War makes her a memorable giant in American history.

Since faith includes risk, Tubman is the quintessential example. Her bold faith should be emulated if we desire to transform the world around us. Looking back on her experiences, Tubman said, "I had reasoned this out in my mind; there was one of two things I had a right to, liberty or death; if I could not have one, I would have the other."[11] Tubman's bold faith inspired others to take the dangerous journey with her to freedom. She told them, "If you hear the dogs, keep going. If you see the torches in the woods, keep going. If there's shouting after you, keep going. Don't ever stop. Keep going. If you want a taste of freedom, keep going."[12] These words should inspire us to keep struggling for freedom, justice, and democracy, the touchstones of our nation. When we fail to have bold faith like Tubman, we postpone making our nation a more perfect union, the world a better place in which to live.

Another person who demonstrated bold faith is Viola Liuzzo—a white thirty-nine-year-old mother of five who left her family in Detroit and drove to Alabama to participate in the march for justice and equality. Liuzzo put her life in danger by helping to ferry protesters in her car because she believed in American democracy. It is certain she knew the risk, but her bold act of faith says she was willing to challenge the structure of evil that held Jim Crow in place. Her bold act of faith also says not everybody in America is filled with hate and bigotry. We are all God's children, regardless of the color of skin. We must stand up and struggle against wrong, evil, and injustice and recognize the full equality of all people. "We must do this, not because it is economically advantageous, although it is; not because of the laws of God command, although they do; not because people in other lands wish it so. We must do it for the single and fundamental reason that it is the right thing to do."[13]

Finally, "any person who questions the grounds of the society, who raises a primary question of human values, is in truth a disturber of the peace and a troublemaker. Such an accusation is entirely correct. Most often men do not want to be troublemakers. Rauschenbusch use to tell his students that there are many good people in the world but there are a very few who are good enough to disturb the devil."[14] Patrick Henry, William Lloyd Garrison, Frederick Douglass, Harriet Tubman, Rosa Parks, Martin Luther King Jr., Viola Liuzzo, and many others were willing to disturb what the devil was doing in American society. Although it cost some people their lives, they were willing to give it on behalf of justice and righteousness. Viola Liuzzo was the only white woman to lose her life in the civil rights movement. Our nation and the world are in need of great personalities who are willing to demonstrate bold faith in the midst of glaring injustice and gross inhumanity to create a world freer and more humane. It takes bold faith to trouble the waters in order to transform our nation and the world for the kingdom of God.

How bold is your faith? Is it bold enough to transgress set boundaries? Is it bold enough to step out of security into insecurity for Christ? Is it bold enough to comfort the afflicted and afflict the comfortable? Is it bold enough to speak truth to power and stand with the powerless? Is American Christianity bold enough to break with ideologies, philosophies, and polices that often protect social and economic inequalities? Until American Christianity is willing to break from the racial and economic rationalization that created the balkanization of racial identification in the American imagination that formed institutional discrimination, it will never be justified before God. It takes bold faith to disconnect from reducing Christianity to only soul salvation while the body, mind, and aspirations of the poor and oppressed are being destroyed in communities of neglect. Bold faith makes the interconnection of religion, politics, and economics. The faith of American Christianity is on trial. The prosecuting attorney of racial, social, and economic injustice has made a compelling case to the jury of justice, equality, and democracy. The question is what will be the verdict? I hope the verdict from Judge Jesus won't be "Depart from Me, you who practice lawlessness (Matthew 7:23)! When we are able to answer these questions, then there is the real possibility of transformation in the nation and the world.

ENDNOTES

[1] Robert F. Kennedy, N.U.S.A.S. "Day of Affirmation" speech, University of Cape Town, South Africa, June 6, 1966.

[2] Paul Tillich, *The Courage to Be* (New Haven: Yale University Press, 1952), 37–38.

[3] Ibid., 39.

[4] Ibid., 7.

[5] Ibid., 8.

[6] Ibid., 36.

[7] Nick Vujicic, *Unstoppable: The Incredible Power of Faith in Action* (New York: WaterBrook Press, 2012), 18–19.

[8] Tillich, *The Courage to Be*, 45.

[9] Ibid., 182.

[10] Patrick Henry, "Speech to the Virginia Convention," *A Treasury of the World's Great Speeches*, selected and edited by Houston Peterson (New York: Simon & Schuster, 1954, 1965), 142.

[11] Sarah Bradford, *Harriet: The Moses of Her People*, e-book, produced by Maria Cecilia Lim and PG Distributed Proofreaders, February 2006 (originally published in 1869).

[12] Flavia Medrut, "12 Harriet Tubman Quotes to Help You Find the Leader Within," *Goalcast* (January 9, 2018).

[13] Kennedy, "Day of Affirmation" speech.

[14] Howard Thurman, *The Luminous Darkness* (Richmond IN: Friends United Press, 1989), 55.

CHAPTER SIX

FAITH & POLITICS

Those who believe religion and politics
aren't connected don't understand either.

—Gandhi

We have a number of serious issues in our nation. Noninvolvement
will not bring about the necessary transformation this nation and the
world needs. There are many people who still believe that politics and
religion don't mix. There are many Christians who are afraid to get
involved with politics. They say politics is too messy and therefore
avoid it all together. Yes, politics is messy; yes, the swamp needs drain-
ing. This is more than enough reason to get involved to help clean it
up. We are affected by what goes on in our government. Policies either
help or hurt people, and most of the time they hurt the poor and the
marginalized. We cannot afford to avoid politics, and religious leaders
should not be afraid to talk about politics from the pulpit when injustice and unfairness affect communities they serve. We must remember
that politics was already at work when Herod ordered the death of
Jesus after hearing of his birth from the wise men. Politics was repre-
sented not only at the trial of Jesus but also at the cross. The forces
of Jewish religious leaders and Pilate of Rome came together in an
unholy synthesis to produce the crucifixion. "It is a commonplace to
say that these same forces—religious, political, social—are operating
still to crucify the Son of God afresh."[1]

Therefore, there is no way we can stay out of politics, because it
involves people, and since it involves people, it involves the redemptive work of Christ. Some Christians believe it is a matter of church

and state separation because Jesus said, "My kingdom is not of this world " (John 18:36). Since Christ's kingdom is not of this world, some Christians believe they should not engage the world for its transformation. James Steward begs to differ: "Do not let us twist Christ's saying, 'My Kingdom is not of this world' into a justification of the pity which removes politics and economics and the way men live in the world out of the orbit of religious concern, and imagines that by this attitude it does God service. It does service to no one except to the powers of darkness."[2] Within our own history, we must remember, had not Christians involved themselves in the political process, America would be much worse than she is. It is a known fact that the abolitionist movement was comprised of a group of Christians who got involved. It is a fact that labor laws were passed because Christians got involved. Social agencies came into being because Christians got involved. Civil rights and voting rights came into being because Christians got involved. We cannot expect to better our nation and the world by avoiding the political process.

> No religion will ever represent the mind of Christ that does not throb with social ardor and go crusading for a better world. No faith deserves to bear the name of Jesus which will not accept the risk, indeed the certainty, of persecution in seeking to translate the doctrines of the Fatherhood of God and the brotherhood of man into the concrete vigorous action of a Christian revolution, as it goes out to redeem the radically disinherited and to establish…freedoms throughout the earth.[3]

Moreover, our democracy demands that we not only speak the truth and stand for the truth but also participate in the political process. Otherwise, our democracy could easily become totalitarian. Henry Nelson Wieman stated,

> If democracy and freedom are to be saved these are the two requirements: Demonstrable truth concerning the common

good which underlies and sustains the diversity of local and private interests but not identical with any part or whole of them; secondly, a form of religion which leads people to trust and commit themselves to the common good sufficiently to allow their government to command resources and concerted action in its service independently of local and private interests. Also, this devotion of religious commitment must control the leaders as well as the people and control those who exercise the power of authority in high positions of government.[4]

We who identify ourselves as Christians and who love this nation and what it stands for must hold our leaders and ourselves accountable. When we stop speaking and standing for the truth and holding ourselves and leaders accountable, then we have lost our democratic way of life.

Those who believe politics is too messy to get involved, here are a few questions to ponder: Did not God send Jesus Christ into our messy situation to bring us salvation? Was this not a case of God involving himself in the politics of humanity to bring about transformation? Was not politics at the trial and crucifixion of Jesus? Did not the Christian movement affect Constantine, who made Christianity the official religion of the Roman Empire? Then how can Christians come to the conclusion that politics is too messy to get involved?

If we truly love our country and the communities in which we live and serve, there is no way we can avoid the political process. God so loved us that he sent his only begotten son right in the middle of the religious and political swamp. God never intended for his people not to get involved in the affairs of those who govern them. Where there is darkness, shouldn't we get involved and shine the light, or should we hide the light under a bushel? "If righteousness exalts a nation and sin is a reproach to any people" (Prov 14:34), how are we going to achieve righteousness unless God's people get involved in the political process? How are we going to have a more just and humane society unless God's people involve themselves? How are we going to have good, fair, and just policies unless God's people get involved? How are we going to have a more perfect union unless God's people involve themselves? Since we are citizens of this nation and the kingdom of God, shouldn't we exercise our citizenship responsibility in both? How can we pray "thy will be done on earth as it is in heaven" and refuse to involve ourselves in the politics of our nation? Our nation is in serious spiritual and moral trouble that could lead to its collapse. How can we sit back and watch its downfall? Will prayer alone achieve justice? Will worship alone achieve equality? Will coming to church alone bring transformation of the social and economic structures of our nation? Did Jesus stay contained in the temple? We all know the answer to these questions is a resounding no. Christians as citizens have a responsibility to help shape society and influence it in the right direction.

The late Robert McAfee Brown, the American theologian and activist, made a profound statement on this subject:

> Any Christian worth his salt knows that in this day and age there is an imperative laid upon him to be politically responsible. When one considers the fateful decisions which lie in the hands of politicians, and the impact which these decisions will have for good or ill upon the destinies of millions of people, it becomes apparent that in terms of trying to implement the will of God, however fragmentarily, politics can be a means of grace.... Politics has become an arena where the most fastidious Christian must act responsibly and decisively if he is not to be a derelict in his duties.[5]

It is our duty to call into question government that crushes the poor, enacts unjust polices, and behaves in ways that cause the people to mourn. We cannot escape this responsibility, especially when any percentage of the people is politically mistreated and or misrepresented.

Whether we like it or not, government is here to stay. God established government, and we should submit to government. However, submission doesn't mean unchecked conformity. Honest dissent is necessary to have good government. There is nothing wrong in trying to have good representation of the people to promote a just and humane society: "Let every soul be subject to the governing authorities. For there is no authority except from God, and the authorities that exist are appointed by God" (Rom 13:1–2). Yes, we subject ourselves to government with the understanding as citizens that it is our responsibility to promote good government by involving ourselves in the political process. Our democratic government is set up as a government of the people, by the people, and for the people, and when the people are wronged by their government, the people must hold government accountable and demand justice. However, should we decide not to get involved in the political process, we deserve what we get. Plato said centuries ago, "The penalty that good [people] pay for not being interested in politics is to be governed by [people] worse than themselves."[6]

Although God established government, it oftentimes cuts across God's will. When this happens, God always sends prophets to warn government leaders to correct their posture, personality, and policies or otherwise come under God's judgment. God warns before God destroys. Moses was sent to Pharaoh; Daniel was sent to Nebuchadnezzar; Elijah was sent to Ahab; Samuel was sent to Saul; Nathan was sent to David; Amos was sent to Uzziah and Jeroboam; John the Baptist was sent to King Herod; Frederick Douglass was sent to Abraham Lincoln; Martin Luther King Jr. was sent to Presidents Kennedy and Johnson. Whenever government goes astray, it causes the people to stray. Whenever government sins, it causes the people to sin. Whenever government crushes the poor, oppresses the weak, and forgets about "the least of these," it causes people to mourn, and God sends his spokespersons to warn the government to chart a new course or suffer the consequences. Fosdick stated, "For to the Christian no human government can ever be the highest loyalty…a loyalty that surpasses the state, the right to be, 'His Majesty's Most Loyal Opposition.' For the Christian conscience and civil liberties are done up in one bundle of life."[7]

We cannot get around engaging politics because it impacts our lives one way or another. The political process is part of the Christian responsibility to win the world to Christ. Voting is a democratic right and a moral responsibility. "A degree of political seriousness, a concern for what is happening to society, an involvement with the way it develops, is the very least we can give. Niebuhr was plainly right. A Christian who does not care about what actually happens in the political sphere, who does not lift a finger to do anything practical about it, is not really a Christian at all."[8] We should not complain to God about the state of the union when we did not lift up our fingers and go vote during elections. We should not complain about what a particular policy is doing to citizens if we are unwilling to participate in honest dissent and get that policy corrected. As Christians we must hear Jesus's words: "Render to Caesar the things that are Caesar's and to God the things that are God's" (Matt 22:21). In other words, exercise your civil as well as your spiritual duty to both God and government. William Barclay was right:

> Christianity was never meant to withdraw a man from life; it was meant to equip him better for life. Christianity does not offer us release from problems; it offers us a way to solve our problems. Christianity does not offer us an easy peace; it offers us a triumphant warfare. Christianity does not offer us a life in which troubles are escaped and evaded; it offers us a life in which troubles are faced and conquered.... The Christian must never desire to abandon the world; he must always desire to win the world.[9]

How do we win the world for God through Christ? One way is our participation in selecting those who govern us. Listen to what Jethro told Moses: "Select capable men from all the people—men who fear God, trustworthy men who hate dishonest gain—and appoint them as officials over thousands, hundreds, fifties and tens" (Exod 18:21). Notice here it says "capable men who fear God," not men who are conservative or liberal, who are good debaters, who are smooth talkers, and who show they can rule with an iron fist, but men who fear God. We should vote for candidates who fear God because "the fear of the LORD is the beginning of wisdom" (Prov 9:10). Candidates who don't fear God will do anything, say anything, compromise anything, and go along with anything. We should vote for candidates "who are trustworthy." Can we trust the candidates who want to hold office to do the right thing even if they have to go against their own party? Can we count on them to tell the truth and stand for the truth? Do they base truth on what God says or what the political party says? Do the candidates have a moral compass? It is our fault if we keep voting for candidates who are career liars.

Scriptures also tells us that we ought to vote for candidates who "hate dishonest gain." Before we vote a candidate into office, we should make sure the candidate is principled. Is the candidate there for the people, or is the candidate there to line his own pocket? We should not have candidates who believe in sending others to prison for inside trading when they are guilty of doing the same thing. Hypocrisy in government must be called into question and held accountable for promoting a double standard. We need candidates who cannot be bought by special interests and who frown upon and hate dishonest gain. We need candidates who don't misuse taxpayers' money all while raising taxes to get more money. Listen again to how we should vet candidates from a biblical perspective and vote for these candidates: "Select capable men [and women] from all the people—men [and women] who fear God, trustworthy men [and women] who hate dishonest gain—and appoint them as officials over thousands, hundreds, fifties and tens." This scripture shows us that God wants us to participate in the process of those who govern us.

Now some might say no candidate has these biblical traits. If this is the case, either you become a candidate or recommend someone who does have these traits. But by all means don't abandon your duty to participate in the political process. Get out and vote, because once we get into the habit of voting and politicians know we vote on a consistent basics, they can no longer take your vote for granted. "The aim will be to create a society in which the weak are protected, the casualties are cared for, everyone has some say in what happens to [them], no one is denied justice or the necessities of life, and everyone feels that he has the opportunity to contribute."[10] Democracy means participation in the kind of nation we desire to live in. Therefore, to sustain our form of government and make it a more perfect union, we must exercise our citizenship rights. It doesn't matter which political party we decide to support. It doesn't matter if we are liberal or conservative; we need both to strike a balance of power. Fosdick says, "It takes two hands on a clock to make it tell time. One goes fast and the other goes slow, but it takes both of them to make a good clock. So it takes the liberal and the conservative temperatures to make a good country and a good church, and the most balanced and wise leader is the man who has both elements in him."[11]

As we move on in this twenty-first century, it is my sincere belief that the hope of the nation lies largely with the postmodern church. Like the government, the church has many problems, but the church still holds the words of life in Jesus Christ our Lord. Regardless of the divisions within the church, God's people must bring to bear faith on the social, economic, and political landscape to produce a better tomorrow for generations to come. We must involve ourselves in the political process as one way to help steer the nation back to God, back to civil discourse, and back to cultural morality. We need local, state, and national leaders to help in this process. Therefore, let us act and pray:

> God give us leaders! A time like this
> demands; strong minds, great hearts,
> true faith, and ready hands. Leaders
> whom the lust of office does not kill;

Leaders whom the spoils of life cannot but;
Leaders who possess opinion and a will;
Leaders who have honor; leaders who will
not lie! Leaders who can stand before
a demagogue, and damn his treacherous
flatteries without winking; tall leaders, sun
crowned, who live above the fog;
(Leaders who desperately work to uplift us all).[12]

Let us remember, God has no eyes but our eyes, no hands but our hands, no feet but our feet, no tongue but our tongue, and it is our responsibility to promote "one nation, under God, indivisible, with liberty and justice for all."

ENDNOTES

[1] James S. Stewart, *A Faith to Proclaim* (Grand Rapids: Baker Book House, 1953, reprinted 1972), 87.

[2] Ibid., 19.

[3] Ibid., 142.

[4] Henry Nelson Wieman, *Creative Freedom: Vocation of Liberal Religion*, ed. Creighton Peden and Larry E. Axel (New York: Pilgrim Press, 1982), 86.

[5] Robert McAfee Brown, cited from P*ulpit & Politics, Separation of Church & State in the Black Church*, Marvin A. McMickle (Valley Forge PA: Judson Press, 2014), 12.

[6] Plato, *Republic*, 1.347.

[7] Harry Emerson Fosdick, *Answers to Real Problems: Harry Emerson Fosdick Speaks to Our Time*, ed. Mark E. Yurs (Eugene OR: Wipf & Stock Publishers, 2008), 220.

[8] Peter Hinchliff, *Holiness and Politics* (Grand Rapids: William B. Eerdmans Publishing Company, 1982), 182.

[9] William Barclay, *The Gospel of John*, vol.2 (Philadelphia, PA: Westminster Press, 1956), 252.

[10] Hinchliff, *Holiness and Politics*, 185.

[11] Fosdick, *Answers to Real Problems*, 210.

[12] Josiah G. Holland, *Light from Many Lamps*, ed. Lillian E. Watson (New York: Simon & Schuster, 1951), 183.

CHAPTER SEVEN

REMAIN FAITHFUL

Be thou faithful unto death, and
I will give thee the crown of life.
—Revelation 2:10

It has been my honest attempt to convince the reader that we must act on our faith to transform the world around us. The battle cry of faith is calling for God's people of all colors and nationalities to act to not only save America but also the civilized world. When we act on our faith, there is no guarantee that things will work out on our timetables. At times we will be disappointed, frustrated, let down, and discouraged because transformation of any situation takes time. However, this is no reason to give up and abandon our efforts. Faithfulness requires that we stick with the task, although in the process we may fall short of our goals. The end results of our efforts are in God's hand, and God has the last word, as he did when he raised Jesus from the dead. We must have patience while acting on our faith. "Let patience have its perfect work, that you may be perfect and complete, lacking nothing" (Jas 1:4). To practice patience doesn't mean to detach from society and not to work for justice, righteousness, and democracy. Patience means to be vigilant, to endure, to press on though at times our nights are darker than a thousand midnights.

I am not advocating a "patience that makes us patient with anything less than freedom and justice."[1] What I am conveying is that it takes time to transform nations and civilizations where wrong, evil, and injustice have had a stranglehold for a long time. It would be wonderful if those in power would straighten up and fly right overnight. Realistically, with most nations this has never been the case, so to struggle for transformation means we must be in it for the long haul. It takes time to accomplish. It took time to transform the Roman Empire to a Christian state. It took time to bring moral change to an iniquitous England. It took time to end institutional slavery in America. It took time to put to rest Jim Crow in the South. It took time to bring down the Berlin Wall. It takes time to accomplish transformation because opposition is there to combat our every effort. This is the reason faithfulness on life's journey is so important. The same forces we struggled against in the past are coming back stronger and more determined to crucify afresh the Son of God and what he represents. Thus, we must remain faithful to our convictions and continue to work to bring transformation.

America and the world are in a moral colossal mess. Evil and injustice are on the rise, and violence is out of control. However, we have a mandate to serve the Lord in this present age by putting our faith in action. James says, "Faith, if it does not have works, is dead" (Jas 2:17). George Sweeting says, "It is ridiculous to say you have faith and then turn your back on every opportunity to demonstrate that faith. If that is how you act, then your faith is not real."[2] Despite the moral crisis we are in as a nation and the world, we have an opportunity to put our faith in action. In turn, Christ is glorified, discipleship is multiplied, the church edified, and the devil horrified. We do a disservice to Christ and his kingdom when we withhold the gospel message in any sphere of life. Christ's birth had cosmic implications. Christ's death and resurrection mean that God's kingdom has defeated the kingdom of sin and the whole world has an opportunity to be transferred from the kingdom of sin to the kingdom of God. But when we stay within the narrow confines of our four-walled church buildings and withdraw from social, economic, and political engagement, souls won't be transferred from one kingdom to another. When people outside the church have not seen or heard much of anything contrary to the kingdom of sin, how can they know about the kingdom of God? Therefore, we should never neglect evangelizing to reach the world for Christ. It is a command of our Lord to go to teach all nations the gospel of the kingdom of God (Matt 28:19–20). We must leave the results in God's hand and remain faithful unto death.

The early Christians lived in a world much like our own. Life and people were really bad. The screws of oppression were tightening; violence and mayhem were at an all-time high; persecution of Christians was an everyday occurrence; the world of politics was a mess; society was just as ungodly and criminal as it is now. Nevertheless, the early Christians preached and lived the gospel of hope, which was predicated on the resurrection of Jesus Christ and fueled by the power of the Holy Spirit that transformed the Roman Empire. The same can be done in this American empire. But "to prophesy smooth things, to preach a comfortable innocuous Gospel that leaves the crying injustices of life untouched, is a denial of Christ every whit as flagrant as Peter's 'I know not the Man.'"[3] When Christians act no different than the world and when they support agendas that are out of line with the kingdom of God, it is no wonder Christianity is dwindling in America. How can Christians say they love God and then look the other way when wrong, evil, and injustice have been practiced on people because of the color of their skin? How can Christians bear the name when racism, prejudice, and classism are so apparent in many churches across America? "The inclusive gospel cannot be shared by an exclusive people. Class-consciousness, racism, and all other forms of prejudice are not consistent with the grace of God."[4] Could this be the reason philosopher Nietzsche said, "If he saw more redeemed people he might be more inclined to believe in their Redeemer"?[5] Could this be why Gandhi said, "I love your Jesus but dislike Christians because they are so unlike their Christ"?[6] We need to look in the mirror and ask ourselves if we are practicing a Christ-less Christianity. One cannot help but agree with James Steward: "The fact remains that the greatest drag on Christianity today, the most serious menace to the Church's mission, is not the secularism without, it is the reduced Christianity within: the religious generalities and innocuous platitudes of a pallid, anaemic Christianity."[7]

To win the world for Christ, Christians must act on their faith—
not just on Sunday, not just when we are around other Christians and
friends, not just when we are in public. Christians must demonstrate
their faith at all times, especially at home and in private. Too many
families have not come to Christ because Christians at home or in
private have shown un-Christian behavior. Too many Christians have
rejected the fellowship of other Christians based on race, class, and
denominational idiosyncrasies. However, all of this can be remedied
through love. Not a love that only shows sentimentalism but love that
shows solidarity with suffering humanity. The priest and the levite
showed sentimental love toward the hurt man on the Jericho road,
but his situation never moved them to solidarity with the man. Therefore, they passed him on by. How often do we sympathize with the
poor, the hurting, the marginalized and the paralyzed of society but
won't get into solidarity with them to help change their reality? The
problem of our nation that produces injustice, poverty, social and
economic inequality is structural. It is not enough to improve the
bricks of society; we must work to rearrange the bricks to have a just,
fair, and equitable society. This is the challenge of American Christianity. As Christians if we cannot demonstrate love by rearranging
the structure of society then our love is anemic and our discipleship
is immature. Our Christian duty is not to maintain the structure of
society but transform it for the Kingdom of God—this is love at its
best. Jesus said, "A new commandment I give to you, that you love
one another; as I have loved you, that you also love one another. By
this all will know that you are My disciples, if you have love for one
another" (John 13:34–35). It was love that brought Jesus Christ to
us. It was love that caused him to dwell among the publicans and
sinners. It was love that caused him to side with the poor, the weak,
and the marginalized against the oppressor. It was love that caused
him to give his body to the cross, his hands and feet to the nail, his
blood for the remission of sin. Jesus could have stopped the evil forces
by calling down legions of angels, but love caused him to finish the
job of redemption. He laid his life down for us (John 10:17–18).

Are we willing to lay down our lives for his cause? Are we willing to love others of different races, classes, and cultures? Are we willing to participate in the structural transformation of the nation rather than just showing a veneer of religiosity? Until Christians love as Jesus did, our faith will be nothing more than a "sounding brass and tinkling cymbal" (1 Cor 13:1).

This book is not a broad brush implying that all Christians are not following Christ. There are Christians doing the best they can to be obedient to the gospel of Jesus Christ. There are churches reaching across racial, class, and denominational lines to demonstrate unity in the body of Christ. Many Christians are putting their faith in action and engaging the political process to help make our nation and the world better. However, I want them to understand that the problems we face are not going to be easy to solve. There will be opposition and criticism. However, to do what needs to get done requires importunity and tenacity. These are the Christians I want to encourage not to give up and to remain faithful. Your work and sacrifice are not in vain. You may be up against insurmountable odds but don't give up. Years ago John F. Kennedy challenged the nation to go to the moon not because it was easy but because it was hard. He said, "We choose to go to the moon in this decade and do the other things, not because they are easy, but because they are hard . . . because that goal will serve to organize and measure the best of our energies and skills, because that challenge is one that we are willing to accept, one we are unwilling to postpone, and one which we intend to win."[8] The challenge was met and achieved, not because it was easy but because it was hard. If we can send people to the moon, we can certainly transform the social and economic structure of society. Yes, it is challenging; it requires sacrifice and commitment, but it is achievable. Some Christians are tired; some are suffering from compassion fatigue; some feel their work is in vain. But please don't give up! Remain faithful! Continue to let your light shine, "because this light is always and everywhere immanent, ready to reveal itself.... However much human destructiveness can ravage individual lives, communities, and even ecosystems, it cannot destroy the fundamental source of life and, thus, of hope."[9] We are not alone in our efforts to transform the world. As the hymn of old says, "There is a Balm in Gilead to heal the sin sick soul. There is a Balm in Gilead to make the wounded whole." Jesus Christ is the balm in Gilead, in America, and all over the world. Stay on the battlefield for the Lord! Helen Keller encourages us to"Let our battle cry be: "No preventable disease, no unnecessary poverty, no blinding ignorance among mankind."[10] In the words of the hymn writer Johnson Oatman Jr.,

> So, amid the conflict, whether great or small
> Do not be discouraged, God is over all;
> Count your many blessings, angels will attend,
> Help and comfort give you to your journey's end.[11]

ENDNOTES

[1] Martin Luther King Jr., *Stride Toward Freedom* (San Francisco: Harper & Row, 1958), 62.

[2] George Sweeting, *Faith That Works: A Study of the Book of James* (Chicago: Moody Press, 1973, 1983), 65.

[3] James S. Stewart, *A Faith to Proclaim* (Grand Rapids: Baker Book House, 1953, reprinted 1972), 19.

[4] Ibid., 56.

[5] John MacArthur, *The Heart of the Bible*, Thomas Nelson Publisher, 2005, 121.

[6] Frank Raj, "Gandhi Glimpsed Christ, Rejecting Christianity As A False Religion," Washington Times, December 32, 2014.

[7] James S. Stewart, *A Faith to Proclaim* (Grand Rapids: Baker Book House, 1953, reprinted 1972), 31.

[8] John F. Kennedy, Address at Rice University, September 12, 1962.

[9] Paul Rogat Loeb, *Soul of a Citizen Living with Convictions in a Cynical Time* (New York: St. Martin's Griffin, 1999), 335–36.

[10] Helen Keller: Her Socialist Years, Edited, with an introduction by Philp S. Foner, Digitized by the Internet Archive in 2016 (American Printing House for the Blind).

[11] Johnson Oatman Jr., "Count Your Blessings" (1953), *African-American Heritage Hymnal* (Chicago: GIA Publications, Inc. 2001), 533.

BIBLIOGRAPHY

BOOKS

Barclay, William. *The Letters of James and Peter.* The Westminster Press, Philadelphia, PA, 1958.

———. The Gospel of John, vol.2 (Philadelphia, PA: Westminster Press), 1956.

Barth, Karl. *The Christian Life, Church Dogmatics, Volume IV,* Part 4, (Grand Rapids: William B. Eerdmans Publishing Company , 1981.

Blassingame, John W. & John R. Mckivigan Editor, *The Frederick Douglass Papers Series One: Speeches, Debates and Interviews, Volume 5,* Yale University Press, 1992.

Bradford, Sarah. *Harriet: The Moses of Her People.* Ebook. Produced by Maria Cecilia Lim and PG Distributed Proofreaders. February 2006 (originally published in 1869).

Brown, Robert McAfee, cited from *Pulpit & Politics, Separation of Church & State in the Black Church,* Marvin A. McMickle (Valley Forge, PA: Judson Press), 2014.

Buber, Martin. *Hasidism.* New York: Philosophical Library, 1948.

Cox, Harvey. *The Secular City.* New York, The MacMillan Co., 1968.

Douglass, Frederick. *The Frederick Douglass Papers, Series Three, Speeches, Debates, and Interviews,* Volume 3:1855-63, ed. John W. Blassingame and John R. McKivigan (New Haven: Yale University Press), 1985.

Fosdick, Harry Emerson. *The Hope of the World.* New York: Garden City Books, 1953.

———. *Answers to Real Problems: Harry Emerson Fosdick Speaks to Our Time,* ed. Mark E. Yurs (Eugene, OK: Wipf & Stock Publishers), 2008.

Freire, Paulo. *Pedagogy of the Oppressed.* New York: The Continuum Publishing Company, 1993.

Garrison, William Lloyd. *The Words of Garrison: A Centennial Selection (1805–1905) of Characteristic Sentiments from the Writing of William Lloyd Garrison.* New York: Riverside Press, 1905.

Harkness, Georgia. *Understanding the Christian Faith.* Nashville: Abingdon-Cokesbury Press, 1947.

Haskins, Henry Stanley. *Meditations in Wall Street.* New York: William Morrow & Company, 1940.

Hazell, Curl Oral. *Real Faith in Action: The Demonstration of Nine Principles that Characterize Authentic Faith.* Eugene OR: Wipf & Stock Publishers, 2009.

Hinchliff, Peter. *Holiness and Politics.* Grand Rapids: William B. Eerdmans Publishing Company, 1982.

Holland, Josiah G. *Light from Many Lamps.* Edited by Lillian E. Watson. New York: Simon & Schuster, 1951.

Hudson, Winthrop S., ed. *Walter Rauschenbusch: Selected Writings. Sources of American Spirituality.* Mahwah NJ: Paulist Press, 1984.

King, Martin Luther Jr. *Stride Toward Freedom.* San Francisco: Harper & Row, 1958.

———. *Strength to Love.* Philadelphia: Fortress Press, 1963.

Loeb, Paul Rogat. *Soul of a Citizen Living with Convictions in a Cynical Time.* New York: St. Martin's Griffin, 1997.

Murray, Andrew. *With Christ in the School of Prayer.* Virginia Beach: CBN University Press, 1978.

Niebuhr, Reinhold. "Christian Faith and Natural Law," *Christian Social Teaching,* complied and edited by George W. Forell (Minneapolis: Augsburg Publishing House, 1966.

Peterson, Houston, ed. *A Treasury of the World's Great Speeches.* New York: Simon & Schuster, 1954.

Prochnow, Herbert V. *The Speaker's Book of Illustrations.* Grand Rapids: Baker Book House, 1974.

Stewart, James S. *A Faith to Proclaim.* Grand Rapids: Baker Book House, 1953.

Sweeting, George. *Faith That Works: A Study of the Book of James.* Chicago: Moody Press, 1973, 1983.

Thurman, Howard. *Deep River and the Negro Spirituals Speaks of Life and Death.* Richmond IN: Friends United Press, 1975.

———. *The Luminous Darkness.* Richmond IN: Friends United Press, 1989.

Tillich, Paul. *The Courage to Be.* New Haven: Yale University Press, 1952.

———. *Dynamics of Faith.* New York: Harper & Row, 1957.

Tozer, A. W. *Man: The Dwelling Place of God.* San Francisco: Fig Publisher, 2012.

———. *Paths to Power: Living in the Spirit's Fullness.* Chicago: Moody Bible Institute, 1940.

Washington, James Melvin. *A Testament of Hope, The Essential Writings of Martin Luther King, Jr.* San Francisco: Harper & Row, 1986.

Wentzel, Fred D. *Epistle to White Christians.* Philadelphia: The Christian Education Press, 1948.

Wieman, Henry Nelson. *Creative Freedom: Vocation of Liberal Religion.* Edited by Creighton Peden and Larry E. Axel. New York: Pilgrim Press, 1982.

Vujicic, Nick. *Unstoppable: The Incredible Power of Faith.* New York: WaterBrook Press, 2012.

SPEECHES

Frederick Douglass, "The Meaning of the 4th for the Negro," Rochester, New York, July 5, 1852.

Patrick Henry, "Speech to the Virginia Convention," Richmond, Virginia, March 23, 1775.

Robert Kennedy, N.U.S.A.S. "Day of Affirmation" speech, University of Cape Town, South Africa, June 6, 1966.

Martin Luther King Jr., "I Have A Dream" speech, Washington, D.C., August 28, 1963.

Abraham Lincoln, "House Divided" speech, Springfield, Illinois, June 16, 1858.

ARTICLES

Hannah More, "Thoughts on the Importance of the Manners of the Great to General Society, and an Estimate of the Religion of the Fashionable World," London: T. Cadell and W. Davies, Strand, 1809, (Hard Press Publisher, Miami, FL), 2017.

Herbert Sclossberg, cited from www.victorianweb.org/religion/herb5.html, Evangelical Movement in the Church of England, part five of "Religious Revival and the Transformation of English Sensibilities in the Early 19th Century."

Diane Severance, "Evangelical Revival in England," *Christianity.com*, Timeline 1701-1800, First published, April 28, 2010. http://www. christianity.com/church/church-history/timeline/1701-1800/ evangelical-revival-in-england-11630228.html

CPSIA information can be obtained
at www.ICGtesting.com
Printed in the USA
BVHW040212260221
601191BV00016B/579